CW00376843

Life in th

By

Tom Hill

Copyright © 2022 Tom Hill

ISBN: 9798808396142

All rights reserved, including the right to reproduce this book, or portions thereof in any form. No part of this text may be reproduced, transmitted, downloaded, decompiled, reverse engineered, or stored, in any form or introduced into any information storage and retrieval system, in any form or by any means, whether electronic or mechanical without the express written permission of the author.

Life in the Max

Dedicated to Mum and Dad,
long gone but not forgotten.
Daughter Casey and my brother Nick.
Also my wife Coral, without whose
help this project would still be two handwritten
exercise books sitting on the kitchen table.

...

Welcome to Hell

That's what I heard them sing
Oh we're so happy that you're here today

There's a warden waiting to meet me
As I make my way inside of the jail
He smiles at me ever so sweetly
And sends me on route to my cell

Grins all up on their faces
Lookin so delighted I'm here
Murders, robbers and rapists
All shouting up in my ear
Welcome to Hell

(Plan B. *The Defamation of Strickland Banks*)

...

Prologue

We would rush home from school every Tuesday lunchtime to catch the top twenty run-down on Radio 1. It was the official chart for the week, not to be missed, with the all-important number one record being announced and aired at one o'clock.

This Tuesday would be different however. As we rounded the corner at the junction of our street, we were confronted by a large navy-blue Bedford flatbed coal lorry. The driver and his mate were sat together on a low garden wall simply gazing ahead in silence, lost in their thoughts and clearly in shock. Their faces were covered in coal dust only exposing their red eyes. They wore heavy donkey jackets. A policeman was stood beside them, another directing traffic around the accident.

We gathered on the corner with some other lads from our school surveying the scene. Apparently, an ambulance had been called but it was clearly too late. A grey blanket covered the body lying dead directly in front of the lorry, his mangled push bike cleared to the pavement. We all knew the victim due to his customized 1970s-style ape hanger handlebars. He was just fourteen years old and in my school year.

This was my first real experience of tragedy close up. It wouldn't be my last!

Career Opportunities

Not one single person that I know set out to be a prison officer. I certainly didn't. It's not something you choose to do. The majority, as I did, simply fall into the job. Perhaps the reason for this is that the public know little or nothing about Her Majesty's Prison Service. Sure, they know all the build-up, the murder, the manhunt, the trial and ultimately the sentence. Then it stops and in time forgotten. The reality is that the men and women who commit crime sometimes pay with life sentences. The average life sentence is around eighteen years, with many sentences exceeding twenty-five years and some serving whole life tariffs. These prisoners' backgrounds vary through factors such as race, religion, social standing and medical issues. The list is endless. A prison's population is incredibly diverse. However, if you are over twenty-one years of age and male, you will end up "banged up" in the Big House.

Let's go back to 1986. The yuppies, Porsches, Margaret Thatcher, Madonna – in the words of Harry Enfield, "loads of money" and that's exactly what I wanted. My job at that time, a butcher at Sainsbury's, wasn't paying well, around £7,500 a year. It was adequate for the time but I wanted more. I'd had a number of different jobs since leaving sixth form in Bristol with my somewhat random list of O levels including Roman civilisation and English literature. I had been in the air cadets from the age of thirteen to eighteen, I was actually good at it, the natural progression being a career in the air force. In fact, that was all I had ever wanted to do since I'd joined 1860 Squadron Detached Flight Air Training Corps. Things didn't quite go to plan. I did eventually join the air force in 1978 aged eighteen. I really enjoyed basic training, even managing to pass out as an RAF marksman with the SLR (self-loading rifle). After my driving course in Land Rovers trade training then began. I had a choice between the RAF police or the RAF regiment. I chose the former. Big mistake. I had opted for a career as a military policeman which turned out to be a glorified gate guard with officious and over authoritarian types in it. My

4

career was over before it had even begun. I often think I should have pursued what I enjoyed which was the regiment, paras or marines. I really needed to test myself.

There was a brief period of employment after the air force as a postman at the central sorting office (Old Market, Bristol). After a week's induction I was issued another uniform – a common theme developing. The long mohair overcoat was perfect to wear for the punk/new wave fashion scene that was sweeping across Britain. Even better than the uniform, I soon realised that you were only required to sign on at the beginning of the shift. I was soon working only a couple of hours in the huge sorting office, showing my face, having a sausage sandwich and coffee at breaktime and then knocking off. Soon, I wasn't even having the sandwich. I remember once passing my old man on his way to work – I was on my way back home. He asked me what was going on. I told him I had started the early shift unloading the trains at Temple Meads station. He replied that I had only been gone a couple of hours as he had heard my motorcycle start up. The game was up and the post office eventually got rid of me – but what a great six months! They simply gave me a couple of warnings before finally dispensing with my services.

After exiting the air force, my father was somewhat disappointed as he had served in the RAF during national service. However, his disappointment would fade and turn to anger bordering on rage at my next venture to earn a wage. I told him I was going to be a real policeman. Why would this trouble my old man? By his proud admission, he was a turf accountant much to the approval of my socially aspirational mother. To you and I he was a bookmaker, a bookie, from a long line of bookies including my grandfather. Gambling was illegal until 1962 so bets were done underground in pubs and clubs. This process still tarnishes legal, independent bookmakers to this day. I grew up in the world working part-time as a bookie's runner or boardman from the age of fifteen, so going "straight" as he put it did not sit comfortably with him. He didn't need to worry.

The Assistant Chief Constable of Avon and Somerset Police congratulated me on passing various tests and instructions, welcoming me to the force. He wanted to inform me that after training school I would be posted to a large modern station in (wait for it) Yeovil. I questioned why not Bristol Central where I thought all the action would be and I remember he baulked at being questioned after offering the post. He then sat back down, shuffled some papers from my file and said, "Ah yes, your father is a bookmaker." I looked puzzled. Eventually, he expanded, informing me that my father had to apply for his Gambling and Excise License annually from Avon and Somerset Police. To avoid a conflict of interest, I was to be posted to far-flung Yeovil on the borders of Somerset and Dorset. I failed to see how I could influence any decisions made by the police regarding my father's business. This senior policeman barked, "Do you want this position, young man?" Standing now, I replied, "Yes, sir, thank you."
We shook hands and I left Kings Weston House HQ knowing my new career was, yet again, over before it had started. The old man simply said, "Told you so, son, you can't trust 'um."

He wasn't wrong. After training, which I found tough in its administrational procedures, I finally arrived in Yeovil. I was paired up on the beat with an experienced officer who wore an old Victorian-style issue cape. I'd never ever seen one except in old photographs. Here I was, patrolling with my flat, peaked cap and upturned collar on my Gannex coat.

When I was allowed out on my own, I remember one Saturday evening the radio called for all available officers to attend a disturbance at a local pub. I ran to the shout, arriving only to see it was all over. Even the dog van was leaving. The following day I was on the carpet again, this time in front of the station's inspector. A member of the public had complained that Police Constable 2130 had arrived at the incident spoiling for a fight and looking disappointed that he didn't get one.

Driving home a few days later with the familiar knotted feeling in my stomach, I was seriously considering my future. Who should stop me on the A37 northbound in my yellow Triumph Spitfire? Yep, Old Bill, Traffic Division. They asked me if I had come from the Royal Naval air station at Yeovilton and was I a Matlow? I proudly announced that I hadn't and wasn't, telling them I was one of "them". I even explained that once I had finished probation, I might move into Traffic. I could see their shock and disbelief so I promptly produced my warrant card. They fell about laughing and sent me on my way. When I returned to the station I was back in front of that inspector again. They had grassed me up.

It had been a whirlwind couple of years, full of highs and lows. During this time my mother had passed suddenly and I had had a serious crash with the Yamaha. Just as I was about to return to the police my mate shot me with an air rifle. After an operation to remove the pellet from my thigh, the police interviewed me. That inspector was not going to be happy. Much to Father's delight I resigned before they sacked me.

Now back home it's late 1980 and I desperately needed a job. Enter the supermarket giant Sainsbury's. They advertised for a trainee butcher and the money wasn't bad. I had some experience in butchering from a Saturday job with Dewhurst when I was fifteen and had enjoyed my time there. It was a small store with a friendly, family atmosphere in south Bristol. The meat manager, Dennis, who was a middle-aged man from London turned out to be a great character. Immediately, he took me to the canteen and promptly told me that he and the rather attractive, middle-aged personnel lady (that he thought he had some sway over and so obviously didn't) had offered me the job. I was the only applicant who had worn a suit and tie.

I really enjoyed my time there; the work was physical and rewarding. The best aspect though was the social scene. There were very few men employed at the branch and they were middle aged, so the majority of the staff were women and part-time students. It was party central and I loved it.

Fast forward to 1986. Things had become stale on the work front; wages had stagnated and I was twenty-six. I wanted part of Maggie Thatcher's Britain. I needed property. So, I no longer needed a job, I needed a career that was both satisfying and well paid. Mark told me during a conversation over the butcher's block that he had been to the job centre during lunchtime. He had seen a card advertising for prison officers and best of all they were paying £13,500 which was double our salary. The following lunchtime I sacrificed my regular game of pool and took myself off to the job centre. I avoided the hundreds of cards displayed advertising every type of job imaginable with a reference and phone number, making my way straight to the counter. The lady thought for a moment and produced from under the counter some very dusty information booklets, so dusty in fact she used a cloth to wipe them off. "These were dropped off months ago."

The next few days were spent studying the information and filling out forms. The more I investigated it, the more it appealed. That was it, my mind was made up, I would apply to join Her Majesty's prison service.

I was soon to discover the wheels of government and the civil service move slowly. Eventually, I was invited to take some aptitude tests at HMP Bristol. I was taken through endless locked gates in this old Victorian jail to a classroom. Thirty of us were seated for the written tests. They were multiple choice covering basic maths, English and observation – you had to be quick with your answers. Time was called by the officers conducting the tests, then a list of six names were read out, including mine. I couldn't believe it; we had obviously failed. The remaining students were taken out of the room, the door closed behind them and knowing glances exchanged. Suddenly, the officer in charge, who couldn't contain himself any longer, turned to us and congratulated us all on passing. The relief was huge. I raised my hand to confirm what we had just been told and that the large group taken out had actually all failed. Confirming this, he then proceeded to talk about medical examinations and the ongoing process. I retained little of this information as I was still in shock as to what had just happened. Then came my interview with a panel of three senior rank officers. They interviewed me at length and two questions stood out:

"What do you know of the service, young man?"

"What do you think you would dislike about this job?"

Instantly, 1970s comedy *Porridge* and Clint Eastwood's classic *Escape from Alcatraz* was all that came to mind. I admitted I knew very little. The panel chuckled to each other and said it was a lot like *Porridge* as if sharing some inner secret. The answer to the second question was simple – "Excess paperwork," I told them.

More chuckling. "Don't worry, son, you will only have to fill in a 'nicking sheet'." Great. Happy days!

My appointment as a prison officer was confirmed subject to checks and references. Months went by and I had heard nothing. I called the Home Office. A very helpful civil servant told me not to worry and that the checking process for the "prison lot" via the police took forever. Very reassuring. Eventually, everything came together and I was to start my training at HMP Bristol, 18 January 1988.

HMP Bristol

Initial training would start at a local prison. We became affectionately known as NEPOS, new entrant prison officers. Very imaginative. My "local" was HMP Bristol. We were not issued a uniform for our four weeks training at Bristol. Instead, we were required to wear a suit with a shirt and tie. In the jacket buttonhole we wore a prison service cap badge to identify us which was completely unnecessary as we really stood out in our "civvie" suits, the idea being this was a gentle induction to a life behind bars. Rightly so, as apart from the interview none of us had been on the inside of a prison.

Each morning started with a gym session taken by the PEIs (Physical Education Instructors). There were only four of us so no one escaped a tough workout. I was a fit twenty-seven year old so I really enjoyed this. One or two of the others didn't. I had thought about specialising in this field later in my career if things worked out. I never dreamed it would be over twenty years later. It was very apparent from the start that free weights were very popular in this environment with both staff and prisoners, boxing and bag work as well. This was way out of my comfort zone. I loved running and football, weighing in at a mere eleven stone and standing five foot ten. Where were the badminton rackets?

We would then be escorted to a wing, workshop, kitchen, hospital and segregation unit to observe the prison routine. We had to record our observations and thoughts daily in our school-style exercise books at home in the evening. The whole experience felt like the first week at school, be it a very scary local comprehensive.

A prisoner approached me one morning whilst breakfast was being served.
"Excuse me, boss," were his opening words.
Once I had realised he was talking to me, he went on to ask about my interest in motorcycles. I enquired how he knew I was

interested and he said that from his cell window on the fours landing, he could see the four of us "new screws" coming to the nick every morning. He went on to tell me that he had seen me wear a Team Yamaha racing paddock jacket. This early encounter made me very aware, very quickly, how we were always being watched by the cons.

Lunch was taken outside the wall in the Mess. It was all very civilised and a waiter arrived at the table dressed in his clean whites and then proceeded to take our order. "Steak please, mate."
"Okay, boss, how would you like it cooked?"
It was then we realised that all the Mess staff including the chefs were "Red Bands", trusted low-category prisoners. This was all going to take some getting used to.

Toward the end of the second week we became used to the general prison regime, slop out, breakfast, labour, exercise, lunch, return to labour, tea, association. Repeat.
Suddenly, we were rushed out from the wing to an office and told to stay there. All very odd. After half an hour the training officer returned. He appeared flustered. What he told us came as a real shock. There had been an escape!
Not an attempt, an actual escape. In fact, TWO prisoners had escaped. Wow, this was exciting, though I thought it best not to say. I had only been in two weeks. What drama!

It turned out that the two prisoners had escaped from the prison laundry. They had somehow managed to hide themselves on the inside of a lorry behind several large, industrial-type laundry bags. The vehicle simply drove out of the prison onto the Gloucester Road, Horfield. The prison was immediately locked down, though it wasn't clear when the escape had happened. We were quickly rushed off to the gatehouse to be sent home early and told to report back in the morning. I was buzzing.

11

It was all over the local news. Dad produced the *Bristol Evening Post* with its headlines carrying the details of the escape. He was asking me questions, but in truth the newspaper knew a lot more than I did. The two escapees were both serving lengthy sentences and the public were warned not to approach them.

The next day the jail was buzzing with activity and there were police vehicles and prison dog units in the car park. A place that had seemed very organised, calm and relaxed now appeared busy and edgy overnight. I was secretly enjoying it all, thinking does this happen all the time? I now know of course that it doesn't and that the prison governor would have faced some tough questions.

The two prisoners were recaptured a few days later by the police, and for us at least things returned back to our new norm. With our exercise books full, fitness levels improved and a minor insight to prison life, we were dispatched to Wakefield Prison Service Training College in Yorkshire after the weekend off. I couldn't wait. I was hooked.

Wakefield Training College

Wakefield Training College made "screws" and Newbold Revel in Rugby "officers". So that was it, the die was cast. I was to be a screw after nine weeks' training in Yorkshire.

The prison service in the late 1980s was mass recruiting staff to introduce what it termed "Fresh Start". The basis of their plan was to reduce the huge overtime bill that the service was incurring year upon year across the prison estate. This involved increasing the officers' basic wage considerably. However, their overtime would be slashed. The vast majority of officers around the country at that time were working seventy to eighty hours per week, every week, in effect writing their own pay cheques. Oh, there was a new black uniform too.

Bags packed, I hitched a ride with Tony in his old gold Mark 4 Cortina up the M5 northbound. The training college, not to be confused with Wakefield Prison which was located in the town, was a purpose built site very much like a military training camp but without the rifle range. Single accommodation with communal bathrooms on each landing was basic. Unlike military accommodation, we didn't have to clean it. We were a mixed bunch, around one hundred and fifty recruits at different stages of training. Our intake was around thirty, including four female officers.

In the classroom introductions were made. The staff were experienced, confident individuals. The trainees were a real cross section from all walks of life and experiences with ages ranging from twenty-one to fifty.

Uniforms were issued, a new black design. Army-style jumpers, peaked caps and a number one dress uniform. We all admired ourselves. Then the girls walked in and we fell about laughing. A-line skirts and old-fashioned style police hats. What really stood out, though, was their uniform was a light blue colour. The prison service had not got around to changing the old-fashioned uniform to match ours. So, with what looked like two different organisations we gathered on the parade square. Drill was a feature of the course; it was being questioned as to its value in the modern service. Personally, I think it was a positive. It helped us bond in a more effective way than the classroom environment, particularly as half of us could drill while the other half had no idea. There were plenty of ex-military only too willing to offer advice. We even had a guardsman who had been at the palace – hilarious.

The classroom was fun and interesting, unlike the military. Opinion and debate were encouraged. The instructors would often include their operational experiences. What was becoming clear very quickly was that prisons differed greatly from their role or purpose to their regime.
"Don't work with YPs (young persons). You'll be rolling about all day," was a quote often offered.
Any adult male under twenty-one was a YP or borstal boy and that seemed to spell trouble with a capital T.

Discussion was endless during the early part of the course as to where and what type of establishment we would be posted to. Even the north/south economic divide of the eighties came into play. One lad was going to sell his house in London if he was posted to the north and "buy up an entire terrace in Leeds or Liverpool."
Others fancied relocating to Wales for similar reasons, however, it soon became clear that with only a handful of jails like Cardiff, Swansea and Usk that wasn't going to happen anytime soon. Everyone was brought down to earth when it was announced that the majority of us would be posted to Brixton or Wormwood Scrubs, as that was where the shortages were most acute.

My mate Wayne was super excited as he had a flat around the corner from the Scrubs. Furthermore, Scrubs were offering quarters accommodation at a hugely reduced rent. He was keen for me to go there as well, the bright city lights of London. It appealed as we were both single – well, I was, sort of. Deep down, I had only ever wanted to work in a maximum security establishment with lifers and long-term determinate sentences. I had always had an unhealthy interest in armed robbery and with the characters that moved in that criminal underworld. In short, I wanted to work with "real criminals" as I saw them. There were conflicting views as to whether I would be allowed to go straight to such an establishment or have to serve two years at a lower category jail first. We would all just have to wait and see where we would end up around the country – as long as it wasn't Wales.

Back in the classroom we learnt about searching, escorts to courts, hospitals, funerals and other establishments, security and report writing. There was a lot of time spent on verbal and non-verbal communication skills. This was a new initiative for the service and was clearly viewed with some suspicion by some who preferred a more authoritarian approach.

Each day we would be on the mats for C&R (Control & Restraint training.) Again, a relatively new way of controlling refractory prisoners and we were told it was a far better version than what the police were using. It soon became apparent that C&R training was intense and a large part of the training programme. That didn't bode well. What made matters worse was that I wasn't very good at it. I had always been a little dyspraxic and it really showed here. I was bending wrists and arms this way and that, much to the amusement and sometimes pain of my colleagues.

The social side of the course was excellent. We were treated like adults and as long as we could stand to attention the following morning on the parade square all was fine. Every Thursday night in Wakefield was epic, Bros was number one with "*When will I, will I be famous?*" and after the pubs we would hit the clubs en masse. Casanova's, I remember, was a favourite haunt of mine. It wasn't just prison staff either, the private cleaning and catering staff from the college would join the fun along with gangs of nurses from Pinderfields Hospital.

15

Well it was the 1980s and I was looking for my Madonna – I thought I had found her the following week. A pretty girl called Marcia had been back squadded due to an injury she had sustained in an earlier course during a C&R session. Chatting to her during the morning coffee break, she told me she was a keen runner. I saw this as my opportunity to encourage the prison service mantra of team bonding, so I suggested a run the next day before breakfast.

"Great, I'll knock your door at 5am," she said.

Turned out she had run at county level cross-country so I was pushed to the limit around Wakefield town centre the following morning, much to my colleagues' amusement. Marcia proved invaluable later in the course when everyone, me included, went down with man flu. Turned out she had been a nurse in a previous life. Things were looking up.

I had settled into a routine at the college. When the weekly Friday morning exam results were achieved, life was sweet. Before long it was the day we had all been waiting for, the day we discovered our postings. A day of dread for many, we had been asked to submit three choices in order of preference. I had chosen Long Lartin, Wormwood Scrubs and Bristol knowing full well I wouldn't stand any chance of number three. My theory was that this would increase the chances of one and two. We were told that after lunch all would be revealed. During lunch you could cut the tension with a knife. It was easy for me, no ties, no commitments, and besides, nobody wanted to go where I did. When we returned to the classroom they couldn't have heightened the drama if they tried. Individual, official-looking brown envelopes were strategically placed on each desk. I opened mine. Result: HMP Long Lartin, maximum security – choice number one! Others were not so lucky and there were a few tears. Wayne had got the Scrubs so we were going to celebrate that evening, whilst others were going to call their families with the bad news.

The following Thursday lunch time I dashed out into town. I wanted a new top for that evening's night out. When I returned

16

to the college the receptionist informed me that two gentlemen were waiting for me in the bar. They had travelled up from HMP Long Lartin to see me. Wow! I rushed to find them, not wanting to keep them waiting any longer. I needn't have worried, they looked pretty relaxed at the bar. They introduced themselves as Paul the senior training officer and John a residential wing governor. They congratulated me on my posting to Long Lartin, informing me that I was the only recruit they were receiving on this intake, making me feel rather important. After briefly explaining that Long Lartin was a lifers' jail, and therefore pretty relaxed and easy going with prisoners addressing staff by their first names, Paul explained that every Tuesday was "Happy Hour" at Lartin, which meant a two and a half hour lunch break, where all the young lads played sport. Great, I thought. I was puzzled though as to what everyone else did. Then the wing governor, John, who had simply been nodding in agreement with Paul, chipped in that I could even have my car serviced when I was on nights by one of the officers who was a mechanic and worked mainly nights to facilitate this sideline. Fantastic. Am I really going to one of the country's most secure jails?

"Well, we have a long journey back. It's been nice to meet you, Tom," they said quickly finishing their pints, shaking my hand and disappearing.

The course completed, goodbyes, phone numbers and addresses exchanged, it was time to move on. We were all given a week's leave before joining our new establishments.

Arrival

HMP Long Lartin is a category A adult male prison located in a little village called South Littleton near Evesham in Worcestershire. HMP Long Lartin is a state-run prison operated by Her Majesty's prison service and was originally constructed in 1971.

I didn't even know where Evesham was. Dad told me it was called the Vale of Evesham and was famous for its apple orchards and market gardens.
"It's just up the motorway. Go and have a drive around."
Sixty miles later, in Alison's clapped-out Mini, we had arrived in the Vale. Black and white timber framed houses, thatched roofs and what seemed like miles and miles of orchards and greenhouses. Dad was right again. We drove past the jail at lunchtime. There were dozens of officers in uniform wearing their caps, cycling to and from it. Their key chains were dangling down their legs, all very surreal. The jail was in the middle of nowhere surrounded by fields, its imposing walls and razor wire stretching into the countryside. We made more than a few passes of it until Alison became paranoid that the cameras had picked us up. I was keen for one more drive-by but she was having none of it, so it was off to find lunch in Evesham.

During the 1960s several notorious, high-profile prisoners had escaped from jails across the country. Train robbers Charlie Wilson and Ronnie Biggs were on their toes from HMP Winson Green (Birmingham) and HMP Wandsworth respectively. Russian spy George Blake escaped from Wormwood Scrubs in 1966 and fled to the Soviet Union. These and other escapes were proving an ever-increasing embarrassment to the government, so they commissioned a report by Earl Mountbatten. His report recommended that all prisoners be categorised either A, B, C or D according to their escape risk, security risk and danger to the general public. Mountbatten also proposed to house those most dangerous category A prisoners in one fortress-style prison on the Isle of Wight, similar to Alcatraz off San Francisco, USA. However, following the Sir Leon Radzinowicz report in 1968, it was decided not to put all of the "bad eggs" in one basket, as Mountbatten had suggested, but to disperse them around the country. Hence the creation of seven dispersal prisons. In this way, prisoners could be dispersed within any of the seven super secure locations. Mountbatten's categorisation of male prisoners was adopted. The original seven prisons were to be Albany, Parkhurst, Gartree, Wakefield, Hull, Durham, and Long Lartin.

While I was researching and checking my facts for the previous paragraph, I found an interesting and informative article written by Simon Price (serving prisoner). Simon and I had many a conversation on the landings at Lartin, putting the world and prison service to rights. If you ever read this Simon, thank you for the information.

My week's leave over, it was time to head back to the Midlands and start work for real. Early one Monday morning in May 1988, I fired up the Cortina Ghia, full of neatly pressed white uniform shirts hanging in the back, and left Bristol.

Come On In

It had been prearranged that an officer called Ken would meet me at the gate and take me to my digs in his house in what turned out to be a pretty village halfway between the jail and Evesham. Handy. Ken turned out to be a fountain of knowledge and very helpful, that was when you could understand him through his thick Scottish accent. His family made me very welcome and I was soon out having a beer with his son Phil. It was common practice for officers to take in probationers. The Home Office had begun to sell off prison quarters so officers could purchase them at discounted prices. There were two prison housing estates, either one affectionately known as "the patch". They were both within walking distance or the preferred option, cycling distance, to the jail.

I entered the "Big House" full of trepidation and excitement. My place of work for the next three or four years would be Foxtrot or "F" Wing with the first year being a probationary one. At this time Long Lartin had six identical wings, A to F, built in the infamous H block style. Each wing had three landings known as the Ground Floor or ones, twos and the threes. There was a large recess in the centre of each landing that housed the ablutions. The landings were closed unlike their Victorian counterparts. On the ground floor were the wing offices, a hot plate area, laundry and the prisoners' kitchen. Prisoners were permitted to buy food and cook meals. This was a long-term lifers' jail after all. On the twos landing would be the "cleaning cupboard", in truth, a large cleaning store, full of equipment to maintain the wing. An association room housed a TV and video machine, boxed in on the far wall. All category A prisoners were held on the twos with a red cell card on their cell door denoting their category. Each wing held a maximum of seventy-five prisoners. At any one time around twenty-five would be cat A, the remainder cat B and occasionally one or two cat C's awaiting transfer. Category A prisoners are held in high security prisons, who, if they were to escape, pose the most threat to the public, the police or national security.

Category B prisoners are those who pose a risk to the public but may not require maximum security conditions, but for whom escape still needs to be made very difficult.

Long Lartin held approximately four hundred and fifty prisoners, serving five years to life, a third of whom would be serving a life sentence.

F Wing

"Fraggle Rock is what they call this wing, we have most of the nonces on here," Officer Bob casually told me.

"Oh," was my response, not really being sure what to say.

He then talked at great length about how he was also a retained fireman, and how he was often called out to a "shout" at the jail.

"I even turned up on this wing once. Fancy, my own wing! We had a laugh that day, I can tell you."

"I bet," I replied, wondering how he could fit it all in.

They were a mixed, friendly bunch offering all sorts of advice.

"Learn all the names, Boyo. Cat A's first," Gerry and Pete said almost in tandem. They were like a Welsh double act from Cardiff, about my age.

"What were you in?" questioned Jim. Before I could answer he told me he had served as a "red cap" in the army Royal Military Police. This question drew the attention of the other officers. I could tell it mattered to them. The service attracted and actively recruited ex-military.

I replied to Jim and the group, "Six years air cadets, flight sergeant."

There was a pause then howls of laughter in which Jim nearly choked on his roll-up, dropping ash down the front of his uniform.

"Best get the brews on then, young'un. Make a list."

"Alright, Jim."

The senior officer of the day in charge of this motley crew was SO Bill. His first question to me was why I was wearing a white shirt.

"Only senior officers wear white shirts," he said sternly. I told him it was part of the new uniform and all officers would now be issued with them. He seemed satisfied. I had already noticed the varied uniform worn. The majority of staff had a mix and match approach of both the old and new style. All officers still wore blue shirts. Ties, trousers, caps and jumpers were a mixture of light blue and new style black; every combination of uniform was on display. SO Bill then went on to tell me that he wouldn't be with us long as he was going on "long-term sick" in a few days, triple heart bypass. Bloody hell, I thought. It must be the roll-ups he was continually smoking.

"Yeah, and the stress of running F Wing. Don't worry, SO Tony is in charge tomorrow, you'll like him," said Officer Bob.

Trafficking

Officer Phil, who was massive, said that I would need a locker for my kit and uniform. He would instruct a wing prisoner called Frage to go with me to the Light engineer's workshop to swap the locks over on an existing locker in the wing staffroom. Frage, real name Fragely, was summoned to the wing office by a loud tannoy system. Promptly, a short, stocky prisoner turned up. "Yes, guv?" he said in a broad Brummie accent. Instructions were given by Big Phil to empty a large, six feet tall metal locker. "Get it over to the workshop with the new screw." Frage set to work.

"What about all of the uniform and kit inside?" I asked. Big Phil told us that it all belonged to a screw who had recently been caught trafficking and wouldn't have the nerve to claim it.

We had been told at training school that trafficking was an ever-increasing problem in the service. We must be constantly on our guard, especially in dispersals where some prisoners have both time and money to exploit vulnerable staff open to corruption.

Good God, a bent screw already – and on my wing. I told Frage to throw the contents of the locker into bin bags, which he did. He then threw the bags on top of the lockers. We then went to the workshop, Frage showing me the way, me unlocking manual gates and electronic steel doors, him carrying the locker on his shoulder. We pass an officer in the corridor. "Well done, son, always make sure the con does the manual labour." I nodded in acknowledgement and Frage grunted, "Guv," under his breath. Outside now, across the exercise yard to the workshops. We entered the light engine shop, which was like a small engineer workshop on the outside. Some prisoners were working, welding and making prison gates. Others were sitting around chatting or playing cards. Two officers and a civilian instructor in a white coat, which made him look like a school metalwork teacher, introduced themselves. Two prisoners quickly changed the locks under Frage's close supervision.

Back to F Wing with my locker firmly in place, another brew in hand, I was beginning to feel at home, part of the team.

The following morning I arrived on the wing at 7.30am sharp, although you were allowed an additional fifteen minutes from the gate to draw keys, radio and handcuffs. Something to do with, Fresh Start, Bulletin 8 and the Prison Officers Association (POA). When I entered the staffroom it was full of officers, some of whom I had met the previous day. There was a short, stocky SO frantically trying to get into my locker with his keychain.

"Excuse me, sir, that's my locker." He ignored me. The locker was now rocking under the force of him trying to open it. I took out my new key, muscled my way around him and opened it. He spun around.

"Who the fucking hell are you?" he screamed at me in a northern tone.

I leapt to attention.

"Probationary Officer Hill, sir."

"Whose is all that stuff in my locker?"

"Mine, sir."

"Where's mine?" he barked.

The penny suddenly dropped.

"Up there, sir," pointing to the bin bags.

The other officers were in hysterics. I was stood rigid to attention. The now very angry SO grabbed a handful of neatly pressed shirts and my number one dress uniform, storming out onto the ground floor landing, heading to the recess followed by me and all the wing officers who couldn't contain their laughter. He proceeded to throw my kit across the floor with me scampering after it.

"Now get the tea and toast on. I'm Senior Officer Tony, your reporting SO."

Stan and Del

Walking the landings, I met cockneys Stan and Del, both cat A prisoners. They were busy preparing food on the twos for their evening meal. The lads had told me that they ran the wing. I thought SO Tony and Bill did. They both eyed me with suspicion, particularly Stan.

"Why are you carrying that in your trousers?" referring to my old-fashioned wooden truncheon. I muttered something about my protection.

"If it kicks off they'll use it on you. Why don't you carry the rolled-up *Sun* newspaper in there like the rest of the screws?" Del laughed. I felt uneasy.

"Leave him be," Del said in a friendly tone.

"Only joking. Tom, isn't it?" said Stan. The three of us then talked for a while.

It turned out that Del was in for twenty years, Class A drug smuggling, whilst Stan was doing an eighteen year stretch for armed robbery having been moved to Lartin after an escape at Dartmoor. They were clearly career criminals, resigned to their fate of long incarceration. The respect they commanded from both the staff and prisoners was obvious. I tried to remain professional but I must admit I was fascinated by their stories and presence. Stan explained his role as the self-proclaimed wing bookmaker. I told him of my experience in the trade. With a glint in his eye and Del chuckling, he told me that we could go into business together. Feeling uneasy again, I left the landing. Officers Jerry and Dave reassured me that it was fine to have an in-depth conversation with these men. "This is Lartin and that's how we keep the roof on, it's called jail craft," Dave said. At training college they called it "Dynamic Security".

Alarm Bell

"ALARM BELL FOXTROT! ALL STATIONS ALARM BELL FOXTROT!" screeched over the radio. I was there, I had heard the bell ring seconds before. It would still make me jump years later whenever a supermarket checkout bell rang. I ran across the ground floor landing of F Wing, prisoners appearing as shocked as I was. There was a fight at the far end of the first spur. Two prisoners, the McCleod brothers, both huge men weighing in around sixteen stone each. One was attempting to batter his brother with a frying pan. Officers Pete and Jerry "the tafia" were already on the scene, trying to split up the two giants. I dived in trying to grab an arm but all thoughts of my Control & Restraint training had vanished. All five of us were now on the floor. Eventually, we separated them – and the frying pan. Other staff had now arrived, the cavalry. Handcuffs were applied, one brother was dragged off to the segregation unit, the other, who had blood pouring from a nasty head wound, was taken to the prison hospital for treatment. We brushed ourselves down and were told to get a brew before writing a "nicking sheet" for the pair of them. As we left the landing, spur wing cleaners were already busy with mops and buckets cleaning up the blood that was splattered everywhere, including our shirts. SO Tony called me into his office. He congratulated me on my performance.

"Good to see you get stuck in helping your colleagues. That's all we ask. Well done, Tom." I felt elated, particularly as my adrenalin was already running high.

"Thank you, sir."

"You can drop the 'sir' now. Tony will do."

"Okay, Tone," I said, still standing there.

"It's Tony. Now piss off and get me a brew."

Stabbed up.

Weekend regimes at the jail were far more relaxed, a less rigid affair. The cons were on general association (soash) with no workshops or education taking place at weekends. They could cook, go to the gym or out onto the "field", a large open grassed space with a football pitch in the middle. Inter-wing matches were played whilst prisoners watched or walked around the pitch with their peers. Staff would enjoy this detail during pleasant weather, but winter was a different matter. An officer would ring an old-fashioned school playground hand bell after an hour signalling the end of the first session and again at the two-hour mark for the remainder to come back inside to their respective wings.

I had come off the field following the last group of prisoners in, having just watched an entertaining soccer match between my wing and Delta Wing. A full English breakfast prepared by Big Phil welcomed me on my return. SO Tony and I were just finishing off breakfast and discussing the merits of our respective football teams Bristol Rovers and Oldham Athletic when a prisoner appeared, stood in the office doorway holding his stomach.

"WHAT?" SO Tony said, clearly annoyed his breakfast was being disturbed.

"I've been stabbed up," said the prisoner very calmly.

"Let us see," said Tony. The con then walked into the office and up to Tony's desk, removing his hands to reveal a blood-stained T-shirt. I jumped up, Tony remained seated.

"Stop dripping blood on my desk."

The prisoner immediately backed out of the office, trying to stem the flow.

"Sorry, Tone."

"Who did it?" The prisoner simply shrugged his shoulders.

"Get him up to the hospital, Hilly."

Suicide

The previous evening I had been on duty with Officer Steve, detailed the twos landing, F Wing. It was general association. Prisoners had returned from workshops or educational classes, tea had been served, some cons had gone to the gym, those remaining were free to mix on any landing and in each other's cells. Some were wandering in and out of the TV room, others cooking. I was playing table tennis with a prisoner called Roy. He was a fellow Bristolian with a sideline in making wooden jewellery boxes. It helped that he was employed in the woodwork shop as his crafting skills were second to none. Orders would come from all around the prison for his work, even the table tennis bat that he regularly used to defeat me with was all his own work. He was serving seven years for burglary and theft. "I'm only doing bed and breakfast," he would say, a common expression for those serving short sentences.

Officer Steve was reading the newspaper. Roy told me we would play the best of three games as he had "business" to attend to around the wings. I took this to mean collecting money for his craftwork. When he left to go debt collecting, I sat with Steve who was still engrossed in the paper. Prisoners would come and go, exchanging chit-chat with us, or rather me, as Steve had now started the crossword.

It was then I noticed cat A, Barry Rondeau. He was tall and slim in his mid-twenties. He was a quiet, respectful individual, never saying much except a polite greeting with "guv" attached. He kept himself to himself. He could always be found in the gym and was a very fit young man. Back in 1980, he had stabbed a rival football fan to death in an FA Cup replay between Swansea and Crystal Palace. Now Palace fan Rondeau was serving life for murder. He would often shave in the evening as everything was a rush in the mornings and the recess stank first thing due to "slop out". This evening, as always, he was taking great care with his appearance. After a shower and precise shave, a prolonged teeth cleaning session would follow. "END OF ASSOCIATION, ASSOCIATION ENDS," was shouted from the ground floor then bellowed over the tannoy. Officer Steve finally put his paper down.

"Come on, lads, bang up."

I locked up one side of the landing whilst Steve locked the spur opposite. Barry Rondeau was one of the last prisoners to go behind his door on my spur, going into his cell wearing his dressing gown and flip flops.

"Night, Barry."

"Night, guv."

I locked his door and completed the roll check.

The following morning going into the jail I passed night staff going off duty.

"One off the roll last night," one officer casually remarked. I knew what that meant – suicide.

When I arrived on F Wing staff confirmed my thoughts. What I didn't know was that it was one of ours. Barry Rondeau had taken his own life at around 2am that morning, cutting both his wrists and simply bleeding out on his bed. I was shocked.

"Old Bill want to speak with you as you locked him up last night."

"Yep, okay," I replied, not really listening.

Within a few days enquires were completed, the cell was cleaned, repainted and another prisoner had moved in. By the weekend all was back to normal – until the next drama.

Football

Sport breaks down barriers, of that there is no doubt. This was evident at Long Lartin. Football was very popular with both prisoners and staff and charity matches had been arranged with Swansea City, Cardiff City and Leyton Orient FC. In reality, we all knew that they would field youth and reserve players, but the excitement and anticipation was through the roof just like the 1979 film version of the sitcom *Porridge*. There were many similarities, particularly team selection and the actual match between Slade Prison and a team of celebrities. Watch the film.

The Swansea game was to be played inside the jail with a mixed team of staff and prisoners. Loyalties split. I was desperate to be on the team.

The day finally arrived.

There was a fantastic fever pitch excitement as Swansea City FC ran onto our pitch in their immaculate all-white strip. The crowd went mad. Armed robbers, terrorists, murderers, drug dealers and rapists.

Loo rolls were thrown up into the anti-helicopter and razor wires. A very surreal and intimidating atmosphere for the visitors. Central TV were in attendance, even if they were more interested in filming IRA prisoners who were watching the game. I had made the team and was on the right wing. It soon became apparent that their best player was at left back, he was attacking us at every opportunity. Our captain and centre back, Officer Big Nige shouted across, "Get tight on him and man mark."
I did.
"Watch out, mate, he's a fucking rapist," shouted a very quick-witted prisoner to howls of laughter. The young, exceptionally talented full back stepped away from me, visibly shaken. More laughs from the cons on the touchline. I tried to reassure the young man saying that I was staff not a prisoner.

"How do I know?"
We both laughed about it later over a pint in the prison social club. That player was Andy Legg who went on to play for Wales at full international level. Oh yes, the result? – we lost 9-0.

Our next game was a fixture against the police to be played at Worcester. This was of course the staff only team. It was a very warm and sunny day and their pitch and facilities were excellent. We knew they had a good side as did we, so knew it would be a close game. The teams were warming up, us in our dreadful-looking early eighties Norwich City strip when, as if from nowhere, a lad in our kit started running around the perimeter of the pitch at speed. He then ran into the centre circle, threw himself to the ground and began doing press-ups.
"Who the hell is that nutter?" said Big Nige.
I had no idea. Steve explained he had just arrived at the prison and had formerly been in the parachute regiment.
"That explains it. He's been dropped on his head too many times."
The ex-para, having finished his personal warm up routine, sprinted over to us and in the strongest Welsh accent asked what position he was to play. In no uncertain terms Big Nige explained he wasn't, he would be substitute. The Welsh man stomped off to the sidelines and the game began. After about ten minutes on the watch the ball smashed into my privates. Within minutes my left testicle had swollen up to the size of a tennis ball and I couldn't run. Attracting the referee's attention, I explained that I had to go off. He looked puzzled as did my teammates. I promptly showed them all my problem to many sharp intakes of breath. Big Nige called for the mad para to come on but there was no need as he had already taken my place on the wing. I limped off sheepishly.

Someone asked what his name was.
Big Nige called out, "Psycho."
He shouted back, "Davies."
"Yeah, Psycho Davies."

I forgot the pain I was in as I was laughing so much. I soon stopped laughing when Glen, who had played for Wolves, peered into my shorts as I lay on the sidelines.

"That's a twisted testicle. I've seen it before, Tom, it needs sorting."

Reluctantly, I left Psycho Davies and the rest and made my way to the police medical centre on site. Before I knew it I was in an ambulance being blue-lighted, driving past the ongoing match to Worcester Hospital. On arrival I am told they would operate on me straightaway and suddenly the seriousness of the situation sunk in. I woke up in a ward, Nigel at my bedside. He tells me that all went well and we won 2-0 and Psycho Davies even scored.

"Never mind all that, what about my balls?"

"Oh, they're fine."

After my recovery I managed to arrange a match between the cons team and my local Sunday league team who I also played for. SO Phil in security was a big football fan so this helped in the decision. Some of my team were under twenty-one and did not all have photo ID, let alone a passport. We got around it and the game went ahead. Losing 2-1 was seen as a great result for such a young side in an alien and hostile environment. I felt everyone learnt a lot about themselves that day, both the young men and the prisoners benefiting from the positive experience that some will never forget.

Charlie Bronson

There have been many famous, or rather infamous, prisoners held behind bars at Long Lartin during the past fifty years, it's a question I am often asked. The problem is that someone who hits the headlines for all of the wrong reasons is often forgotten or eclipsed by the next infamous perpetrator. Here is a list because I know you still want to know. It's in no particular order and by no means exhaustive. If you would like to know details hit the search engine, it's all there in the public domain.

John Straffen
Steve Wright (not the DJ)
Nathan Matthews
John Cooper
Christopher Halliwell
Abu Qatada
Abu Hamza
Radislav Krstić
Jeremy Bamber
Mark Dixie
Ben Green
Vincent Tabak
Ian Watkins

and

Charles Salvadore, formerly known as Charles Ali Ahmed – better known as Charles Bronson.

The first time I met Bronson was on C Wing. I was on the twos landing with Officer Paul. A Charlie Wing officer had reported sick that morning so I was sent there to make up the roster. The roster that day consisted of one senior officer and seven officers, the minimum staffing levels for the unlock of a residential wing.

Within minutes of the morning unlock at 8am, a prisoner appeared in the centre of the landing. It was Charles Bronson. He was completely naked and covered from head to toe in prison issue black boot polish. Waving a saucepan about his head he shouted about the prison system being broken. Other prisoners were actively encouraging him while the remainder, rightly, backed away. We stood up in an attempt to calm him down and tried to reason with him, but he was having none of it. He ignored us and continued his rant, though more about the Home Office now.

After a little jig he rushed past us and into the association room and proceeded to smash the TV screen with the saucepan, simultaneously throwing the video recorder out the window. He continued to destroy furniture and smash windows. We all withdrew, pressing the alarm bell and telling prisoners to go behind their doors, which they promptly did. Exiting the landing, we locked the steel door thus securing and sealing off the twos. Staff were now running onto the wing as a result of the alarm bell. We stopped them on the stairs and explained what had just happened. It was decided that two Control & Restraint teams in full riot kit and shields would be deployed to enter the landing and restrain him. Officer Paul and I were instructed to place Bronson on governor's report and have a brew. As we finished our cuppa two C&R teams consisting of four officers per team plus a dog and handler arrived on the wing. After a short briefing they entered the landing.
"Long shield up. Visors down."
Bronson was asked to comply with instructions for his surrender to the first team. He refused, throwing the saucepan at the shield. The order was repeated and again ignored. The team rushed at him with the shield, burying him against the wall. After a short scuffle he went to the floor, handcuffs applied. Blanket thrown over him, he had been successfully restrained, or as we called it "flat packed". He was then taken to the segregation unit where he normally resided. He had lasted a mere two days on normal location. C Wing staff and prisoners were glad to see the back of him.

COACD Part 1

I had almost completed my probationary period in the service and things were going well. I was becoming confident in my ability. It was very important to be able to converse with prisoners at all levels regardless of their social standings. I felt I could talk to most, not all, about anything. From their offence to what was for "duff" (pudding) at lunchtime, nothing was off limits.

Principal Officer Jim called me into his office.
"Hilly, I have a job for you," he said in his soft Irish accent.
He told me that I would be going on a week's detachment to Wormwood Scrubs (I could meet up with Wayne). We were to take a high-profile cat A prisoner from our segregation unit to the Scrubs where he would be lodged. We would produce him each day to the Court of Appeal, Criminal Division (COACD) held at the Royal Courts of Justice (RCJ), The Strand, City of Westminster, London.
"Okay, Jim, but you know I still have a couple of weeks left on probation," I said, trying to contain my excitement. Probationers were not allowed to be part of a cat A escort.
"Don't worry about that, you've passed."
Elated and full of confidence, I asked the PO who the prisoner was.
"Vincent Hickey," he replied. I instantly knew who Hickey was. He was one of the Bridgewater Four, convicted of killing a thirteen year old paperboy, Carl Bridgewater, a crime that shocked the nation in 1978.

The convicted men had always maintained their innocence. There had been prison rooftop protests and questions were being asked of the West Midlands Serious Crime Squad. In March 1983, both Vincent and Michael Hickey staged a rooftop protest at HMP Long Lartin. They stayed up there for three weeks. Towards the end of November 1983, after being transferred, twenty-one year old Michael scaled the roof of HMP Gartree in Leicestershire and began what became the longest rooftop protest in British history against his conviction for murder. Remarkably, Hickey's protest would last three, cold, winter months. Throughout the protest, he was sustained only by provisions sent up on lines by his fellow prisoners. At no time did the authorities make an attempt to bring him down.

PO Jim reminded me to pack my number one uniform and wear my peaked cap for the press this time. I had been to the COACD with a Cat B prisoner who had successfully appealed against a sentence a couple of weeks earlier. His sentence was reduced by two years for a robbery by three appeal court judges. It had made *Central News* because of its Midlands connection. PO Jim had been having his tea at home when I appeared on his TV screen at six o'clock without my hat.

Helicopters

A new cat A had arrived on F Wing – Andy Russell. He had made headlines around the world for hijacking a helicopter at gunpoint, forcing its pilot to fly to HMP Gartree. The helicopter was forced to land and fly off again with two escaping cat A prisoners. Stan and Del introduced him to me, he was moving in opposite them. We immediately got along – he had the same musical tastes as me. This was evident when I was rummaging through his CD and tape collection that had just arrived from reception.

Stan said, "That's all down to you, Andy," pointing out of the window. We gathered around to see contractors erecting anti-helicopter defence wires in the grounds. I told the three cons that soon the entire prison would be covered by these defences. There was almost a paranoia now at the Home Office about helicopters. Even the garden works party had been ordered to chop down a beautiful cherry tree in the grounds.

Stan took this opportunity to ask me to help him work out some complicated horse racing and football bets that he had taken. Out from his cell came a big black book that he had acquired from the education department. Our maths wasn't cutting it, even with Officer Robbie using Del's calculator, which I guess had also found its way from education. I told the group that my old man could sort this mess out. Robbie suggested that I phone him, Stan quickly agreed. Officer Robbie continued, "Check with SO Tony first, I'm sure it will be fine."

Stan and I went to the ones to seek out Tony who gave us the go ahead as long as my dad agreed. Stan and I went into the office and I phoned Dad's betting shop. Dad answered and asked if Stan could talk directly to him. I said he could. Handing him the phone, a very respectful, convicted, category A armed robber introduced himself to my father, addressing him as Mr Hill. Very quickly he was calling him Tom Senior. Stan ends the conversation saying, "Nice to talk to you, Tom, yes, speak soon. Bye," and hands me back the phone. Dad tells me what a nice man Stan is.

Searching

The searching of prisoners and cells is an important part of the job. When an officer finds an illicit item, particularly hooch (an alcoholic fermented liquid), drugs, escape equipment, weapons and later mobile phones, they would take credit and rightly so. The possession of these items puts us all in danger. Some of the homemade weapons found in prison would put Rambo to shame. Weapons were manufactured secretly, everywhere in the prison using anything – metal coat hooks, window handles, plastic loo brushes and toothbrushes.

The security department organised the search teams and which prisoner would be searched. My detail was to search after breakfast. I reported to security promptly. SO Phil and PO Mel handed me the paperwork. "A cat A on Delta Wing, he is a known brewer (of hooch) and can be argumentative and aggressive," was the intel SO Phil relayed to me.
"Great, who's my partner?" I replied in a sarcastic tone. There was a pause.
"Sorry, Tom, it's Officer Davies," said Phil in a genuinely apologetic manner. PO Mel just laughed.
"Not Psycho Davies?" I protested.
"Yes, but we're trying not to call him that," said a now sterner PO Mel.
"Did you know he set his hair alight at training school as a dare? And where is he?" There were blank faces. Suddenly the door burst open and there he was, Officer Psycho Davies. He looked like a younger version of Charlie Bronson, even down to his army moustache. PO Mel immediately tore into him about being late and improperly dressed. It was minus six degrees outside and he wore just a short sleeve shirt without a tie. I turned and ushered him out of the office to save any more embarrassment.

We entered D Wing to calls of "BURGLERS ON THE WING" shouted by prisoners who had noted our arrival. This was a customary warning to all that a search team was present. We found our prisoner and escorted him to his cell on the twos. He was surly towards us right from the off. Upon entering the cell an overpowering smell of hooch hit us. Officer Brian, as I was now trying to call him, was already seizing a large reception box from under the bed with the con staring over him. There were gallons of hooch in the box which was now sloshing about, spilling onto the floor due to Officer Brian's enthusiasm. We had hit the jackpot. It was the wing's supply. I opened the cell door and the con stepped outside. Brian attempted to drag our find onto the landing, but he only succeeded to bash it into the doorframe spilling even more. An audience of approximately half a dozen angry cat A's had gathered outside the cell. They were demanding that we put the hooch back and leave. Things were getting ugly. Luckily, I came up with a plan. Brian thought I was going to back down because I told him to drag the hooch back into the cell. The cons appeared happy, Brian did not. As soon as he dragged it back in I slammed the cell door shut with us inside, locked it and radioed the control room for help. The cons were shouting abuse and kicking the cell door threatening to burn us out. We were laughing as we could hear staff and an angry Alsatian coming onto the wing. The door clicked open and there were our colleagues laughing at us.

COACD Part 2

We picked up Vincent Hickey from our segregation unit on Sunday afternoon, travelling to the Scrubs for the appeal court production on the following Monday morning. This was an appeal against conviction that had been granted some ten years after the original sentences were handed down to the Bridgewater Four. Hickey was fully compliant to our requests and soon we had left the prison in a cat A cellular vehicle – or "sweat box" – and were heading for London, on board a driver and his navigator, in the back PO Chris and Officers Charlie, Jim and myself, not forgetting the prisoner handcuffed in one of the three cells. I'd had no dealings with Hickey but it was clear that the PO and other officers had. They called him Vinney and there was a relaxed atmosphere as we handed him over to the staff at Scrubs. "See all you guvs in the morning. Don't be late, I have an important appointment tomorrow."

The next morning we picked him up along with his co-defendants, Jimmy Robinson and his cousin Michael Hickey. They had been transferred from HMP Gartree. We now had a two-car police escort for our cat A van as it sped across London to court. The three co-d's were secured in cells that were in the bowels of the courts. The fourth member of the gang, Patrick Molloy, had died in prison of a heart attack two years into his sentence. The three of them were naturally apprehensive for the week ahead, but they still managed to joke with us about our appearance in our number one uniforms. We left them with their legal teams and went off to have the legendary £1 appeal court breakfast, cooked and prepared by prison officers who manned the courts.

During breakfast we were asked to help out in the dock for a "quickie" hearing of some kind as they were busy. PO Chris agreed as we were not listed to start our case until 11am. We escorted a young lad up to the dock. He was smartly dressed in a suit and tie and in his mid-twenties. We had no idea what the case was about. On entering the secure, bulletproof glass dock, the prisoner waved and blew a kiss to a pretty woman of a similar age. He told us she was his fiancée which would make what happened next all the more shocking. He thought he had been brought to court again for a reduction in his sentence, but it soon became apparent that the opposite was about to happen. The Attorney General has the power to increase a sentence if he considers it too lenient. The young man had been convicted of the rape of an elderly woman. He had threatened her with a weapon and stole money from her house. As the details of the case were examined, the prisoner was shaking his head and muttering that it was all lies. His fiancée was clearly shocked and visibly upset. I wondered if she had been present at the trial and what had he told her?

The judge quickly summed up saying that he considered the original sentence too low considering the age of the victim, the presence and threat of a weapon and that the offence had some degree of planning and premeditation. The lad was told to stand. We stood with him as the judge said, "I will increase your original sentence for the reasons I have indicated, from five and a half years to nine years. Take him down." He was shaking now. We immediately gathered around him to usher him out of the dock via a door behind us, downstairs and to the cells. He looked at me asking what had just happened. I told him that we would discuss it when we got downstairs. PO Chris nodded to me approvingly. As we left, I turned to see the fiancée holding her head in tears.

We all settled into the daily routine of court. There were clearly discrepancies and flaws in the case against the three remaining convicted men. Listening each day to the evidence presented, it was becoming increasingly clear that their convictions could be judged unsound and ultimately overturned by the appeal court judges. The three prisoners were feeling more confident as the week passed. Vinney Hickey and Jimmy Robinson in particular, would openly discuss the case and their thoughts with us. Their legal team was buoyant also. I had purchased Paul Foot's book *Murder at the Farm* (published 1986). He was

42

the *Daily Mirror*'s crime correspondent investigating the case since 1980. He had repeatedly returned to the case as he and his colleagues felt an injustice had been done. Paul Foot was present in the public gallery each day. Vinney had told me to get him to autograph my copy of the book, then he said the three of them would sign it too. I thought it was a great idea. Vinney was flicking through it when PO Chris appeared and told him what we had decided. Chris said, "It would be a little unprofessional, don't you think, Vinney?" The book was handed back to me by Vincent who just smiled. I was disappointed but deep down I knew PO Chris was right.

As the week finished so did the summing up. Confidence was high. We had discussed how we would be travelling back to Long Lartin "empty". When the decision was announced that their appeal had been rejected there was understandable shock from all parties present. Vinney just said, "Take me back."
He didn't even wish to discuss the verdict with his legal team. His cousin Michael was very quiet and showed little emotion. Jimmy Robinson was the most vocal and angry. I told Vinney that for what it was worth, I could not understand how they had come to such a conclusion. We handcuffed him and returned to HMP Long Lartin.

Riot and Attempted Escape

Sunday 1 April 1990

I was out on the field supervising association. It was a pleasant, spring afternoon. John Straffen, dressed in his usual scruffy boiler suit, walked toward me with a small transistor radio pressed to his ear. Straffen, who was on my wing, had killed two young girls in the summer of 1951. He was deemed unfit to plead and committed to Broadmoor Hospital. During a brief escape in 1952 he killed again, this time a five year old girl. He was sentenced to death in July 1952 but this was commuted to life imprisonment as the Home Secretary of the day described him as "feeble minded". Straffen went on to become the longest serving prisoner in the UK. He approached me muttering something about a riot at Strangeways. I told him I wasn't interested and to carry on walking around the field. He walked away, still talking to himself. Staff and prisoners generally tolerated him due to his time served and childlike behaviour, allowing him to live with the general population rather than in segregation. I personally felt that he wasn't as simple as he often appeared, allowing himself a degree of liberty, particularly amongst his peers. His cell on Foxtrot was bare. He had an old-style, prison issue wooden chair, two army-style woollen blankets that were no longer issued, a metal compartmentalised tray for his food, again, no longer issued, and a modest stamp collection. Straffen, completing another lap of the football pitch, was heading my way again, this time almost breaking into a trot.

"What, John?"

"I told you, young'un, the roof is off at Strangeways," he said grinning and holding out his tiny silver radio.

I took the radio from him, putting it to my ear. I realised what he was trying to tell me. There was a full-scale riot at HMP Strangeways, Manchester. Prisoners were on the roof. The school bell rang shortly after and I rushed back onto the wing. The staff were all stood around the tiny TV in the back office. Prisoners had broken out onto the roof and were throwing slates down onto the officers below. These images were shocking.

44

Many of the cons wore masks to hide their identities, but to the outside world they looked and were extremely dangerous. One wore an officer's cap and coat – we feared for our colleagues. It was reported that wings had been wrecked and there were multiple fires.

The following evening, Monday 2 April 1990, I was locking up F Wing ground floor with Officer Steve. SO Tony was stood in the centre of the landing.
"ALARM BELL, CHARLIE WING. ALL STATIONS, ALARM BELL, CHARLIE WING," came over my radio. I shouted to Tony but he told me to lock up my landing spur first before responding. As I locked the last prisoner up my radio blared out again, "ALARM BELL CHARLIE, ALL AVAILABLE STAFF TO RESPOND."
"Tony, all wings are locking up, no one is going," I shouted.
"Go! Take Steve with you, I'll finish up here," replied Tony.
Officer Steve was in his fifties and still had half a dozen prisoners to secure. The threes and twos always took much longer to lock up than the ones. I ran to C Wing with Steve in tow.

As we reached the entrance SO Bob was stood at the open door of the wing with glass splinters all over his thick, military-style jumper. He was physically counting and identifying his staff off the wing. They all looked visibly shaken. No other officers had responded to the alarm bell yet. The noise was incredible and it sounded as if the entire wing was being demolished. Pipes were being ripped off walls, everything was being destroyed. With his staff off the wing, SO Bob slammed the main door shut. SO Tony and a handful of officers had now arrived at the scene. As Tony was attempting to secure the door a few prisoners appeared at the window pleading to be let off the wing. SO Tony told them to go to their cells and "wedge up" or lock themselves behind their doors. We guessed that some of them were nonces (sex offenders) fearing for their safety. They quickly disappeared.

45

We could not allow the disturbance to spread and lose what little control we had. Tony ordered me to run to the centre and bring back a bag that contained heavy chains, padlocks, wooden wedges and a small sledgehammer. I ran through the corridors arriving at the centre. The PO had the safe already open and handed me a hessian sack. We didn't even speak to each other as the urgency of the situation was obvious. When I ran out of the centre and back into the corridors two dog handlers were entering from outside attempting to control their dogs as I rushed by.

Back at Charlie Wing door, I spilled the contents of the sack onto the floor and we hammered home the wedges underneath the steel door. The chains were being wrapped around a corridor gate; it was dawning on me the seriousness of the situation. Do they have keys? What weapons have they manufactured? Do they have a firearm? Suddenly, someone shouted, "LOOK, THERE ARE CONS OUTSIDE!" Sure enough we could see three or four figures outside of the wing. I instantly knew it was prisoners by their distinctive donkey jackets with sky-blue shoulder patches. One of the fifty-two high mast lights that lit up HMP Long Lartin like a birthday cake when viewed from the Cotswold hills was illuminating them. Half a dozen of us were ordered back to the centre. As I ran back for a second time the PO was now stood at the centre's main entrance, both steel doors open. "OUTSIDE. THEY'RE IN THE GROUNDS!" he bellowed. I hadn't seen the two dog handlers so I guessed they had been redirected back outside by the control room which would be monitoring the cameras and controlling the radio traffic. It wasn't called the ECR (Emergency Control Room) for nothing.

As I ran out into the cold night air the chill immediately hit me. We only wore our white, short sleeved shirts so at least we could clearly see each other. The officer running in front of me drew his stave and I drew mine. Running around the wings we had been instructed via the ECR and radio to go to Fence Section 4. This was opposite Bravo Wing and near the halfway line of the football pitch. Coming to a gate by a workshop, the four officers in front of me had stopped. They had unlocked the gate but it didn't swing open because the fleeing prisoners had the foresight to wrap wire around it. An officer was frantically trying to untangle it while the five of us waited nervously. At last he got it open and we ran onto the edge of the association field. As we came onto the touchline of the pitch I could see around a dozen figures by the outer fence that stands eighteen feet high and is topped with double reels of deadly razor wire. Reaching the centre circle, it became clear there were more prisoners than us. Nine in fact – eight cat A's and one cat B whose cell on the ground floor of Bravo Wing had been used to make good their escape by cutting the window bars.

Suddenly, out of nowhere, an all-black Alsatian shot past us. We slowed up to a walking pace, taking in the situation. The dog turned sharply and headed for the fence. We were just ten yards from Fence Section 4 while the attack dog was trying to go through it. I could see that nine prisoners were through and in the sand trap next to the twenty feet outer wall, topped with its anti-escape beak. This was designed to make escape with grappling hooks, ropes, nets or ladders very difficult. They had cut a six feet vertical section of fencing with homemade bolt cutters, peeled it open and gone through, leaving one prisoner, cat A Alec Sears, to pull it back together and cleverly padlock it in place to stop us, and more importantly the dogs, getting through. Sears was throwing what turned out to be pepper from a large container at the dog that was trying its best to get through. A second dog was running and barking madly up and down the fence line, its handler telling us to stand still. We already were. Dog handler Alan struck Sears with his stave. He fell to the ground instantly, his head bleeding heavily. The remaining eight prisoners panicked and two of them got on their makeshift wooden ladder at the base of the wall, but their combined weight caused it to collapse. They had no choice now but to surrender to us. They made their way back through the fence, quietly dragging a dazed and concussed Alex Sears to his feet. They removed their Ku Klux Klan-style hoods, making them appear somewhat less dangerous. I noted Andy

47

Russell was one of the would-be escapees. We just caught one another's glance but said nothing. Surrounding them, dog handler Alan secured his dog and we all stood silent. The other handler was attempting to capture his canine that was barking at anything that moved. A third dog team had arrived now. We moved off the field to locate all nine in the segregation unit.

Inside now and approaching the unit, its heavy, steel doors were being unlocked. There was even a welcoming committee. The prisoners looked nervous. The PO ordered them all to be thoroughly searched, we had seen them throw homemade blades and other items down when they surrendered to us outside. Some of them wore hand painted camouflage tracksuit bottoms and sweatshirts, others had industrial safety boots from the workshops with six-inch nails in the toe to kick out at the dogs. One prisoner handed over a metal bar as he was about to be searched. They were processed one at a time, given a blanket and secured in a cell.

When the last one was located, the PO sent for Stan Thompson to be unlocked and brought to the seg unit. I was puzzled as to why on earth Stan was needed. He was promptly delivered. We discreetly acknowledged each other with a simple nod. The PO handed him a notepad and told him to inspect every captured con, then confirm in writing that they had not suffered any injuries at our hands. He briefly inspected each man, speaking to them through the observation panel of their cells. When he had finished his inspection he signed the document and thrust it at the PO.
"I have done what you asked, take me back to Foxy."
I piped up that was my wing and I would take him back. Stan gave a nod to the PO in agreement. Walking through the corridors we didn't say much. Stan asked if anyone had got over the wall, I told him they hadn't.
"They're making a right mess of Charlie and the IRA have barricaded up on the twos." I had almost forgotten about C Wing with all the excitement outside. I locked Stan up. "Goodnight, see you tomorrow."

48

Stan replied, "Yeah, be careful."

Returning to the centre, I bumped into the excited and slightly eccentric Officer Psycho Davies, who I was warming to each time I met him. We quickly swapped stories, he was at home, a prison quarter on the patch and getting ready for his night shift when the quarter's alarm went off. Most officers had removed this antiquated, electrical alarm system from their lofts when they purchased their quarter. However, in typical Officer Brian fashion, he hadn't. He told me he had run out of his house, over the road, to the prison social club where officers were pouring out and responding to the alarm. They had been directed to White's Farm where they stood outside the perimeter wall, waiting for any escaping prisoners to climb over. They were joined by two dog teams. "We pulled out fence posts to defend ourselves," he said excitedly. This explained why he was still wearing his hat and coat and was extremely muddy. I was trying my best not to laugh.

It was around midnight when I entered Charlie Wing and there was water, broken glass and paint everywhere. It was a mess. Going upstairs onto the twos landing, it became clear there was a barricade halfway down one spur with a handful of prisoners behind it, negotiating with staff. They were IRA. The rest of the wing was secure. It wouldn't be long now before intervention as four C&R teams had arrived, fully kitted up and raring to go. This had the desired effect. Some measure of agreement had been reached and the terrorists, or political prisoners as they saw themselves, were finally locked up. Roll correct – prison secure. Officer Gerry took me home as I had cycled to work a mere nineteen hours earlier. Taking my paint splattered boots off, sleep didn't come straightaway as my mind was racing.

Copycat riots and disturbances erupted around the country, HMP Strangeways and a host of other prisons dominating the news every evening. The following week, whilst watching *News at Ten*, I couldn't believe my eyes. A police helicopter was hovering over HMP Dartmoor. The TV camera zoomed in, reporting that prisoners were about to break out onto the roof as the roof tiles fell away. Then, in the middle of this huge roof section, a prisoner's head appeared in the sunlight. Within seconds he triumphantly began to clamber out. It was JoJo Collins. There he was, stood alone on HMP Dartmoor's roof.

We had only just transferred him there the previous week for being involved in Charlie Wing's riot. He was a young scouser and all the young screws liked him. He was very funny and quick-witted, never laying his hands on us. Don't get me wrong though, he was extremely disruptive. Years later at Lartin, on another sentence, he recognised me in the corridors. It was sad. He was a shadow of his former self, bloated by suppressive drugs (liquid cosh). I had no idea who he was until he told me. Then I recognised that sparkle in his eyes and we hugged. When I made enquiries on Delta Wing where he lived, the staff told me other prisoners would bully him. I was fuming, they certainly would not have done that twenty years ago. Where was the respect?

A five-month public enquiry was held into all of the prison disturbances around the country. This culminated in the publication of the "Woolf Report" chaired by Lord Woolf. He recommended major reform for the prison service which at first we welcomed. Conditions were extremely poor in city "local" jails like Strangeways, Liverpool, Bristol and Cardiff to name but a few. The prison service was, and still is, known as the forgotten service. It soon became clear that the enquiry's recommendations would favour the prisoner. This meant effectively empowering the offender. For example, a grievance procedure was introduced (Request and Complaint Forms) to be completed by the con to complain about anything from the thickness of their mattresses to grievances against staff. This would have to be answered in writing within three working days. They poured in; we were inundated. Compacts and contracts were drawn up for prisoners to sign, outlining our expectations of them whilst in custody. They were not worth the paper they were written on. The balance of power was shifting and not in our favour.

TVs arrived at Long Lartin, one for every cell, rental cost at £1 per week, once electric and two power points were installed. We were very sceptical at first although it soon became clear how positive this innovation was. Prisoners and staff felt safer and the large TV association room on each wing became redundant overnight. They were dangerous places to watch TV or a video when darkness fell. Hooch, drug taking and violence were all too prevalent. Many weak or vulnerable cons would not set foot in there. It would also be intimidating for us at times when you had to manually turn off *EastEnders* before the credits rolled. The dangerous practise of "wiring up" stopped immediately. Before electric, a prisoner's power source for his radio or stereo was batteries. They were an expensive purchase on the canteen list. Every ounce of power would be obtained by laying them on the hot pipes that ran through the cells; fine in winter. The secure light source on the ceiling would be circumvented by burning a hole into the reinforced plastic, running wires down to the radio or stereo. Suddenly, incidents of power cuts and accidental electrocutions fell. The infamous phrase, "Guv, I've been PP9'd," disappeared. A PP9 – putting a large square battery into a sock – was a common weapon. Prisoners were ingenious, but as soon as the pool tables arrived the PP9 was superseded with pool balls. Give them an inch and they take a mile.

There by the Grace of God

Back home in Bristol, Dad's first question was, "How's Stan? Alright is he?"

"Yes, Dad, he's fine."

He disappeared for a moment, returning with a copy of the *Bristol Evening Post*. "I've saved this for you, look, it's on the front page. I bet he will be with you soon," he said, handing me the paper. The headline picture was the Great Train Robber Ronnie Biggs, stood on a beach in Rio de Janeiro, Brazil, with Kevin Rawlings. Kevin had just been convicted of smuggling cocaine into Britain with his Brazilian girlfriend. He had hidden the Class A drug in the young daughter's teddy bear. I was gobsmacked but I guess not surprised.

Kevin and I both grew up in Charnhill, Bristol, a middle-class estate. Our parents would frequent the local Conservative Club. We went to the same school and both enjoyed football, but that is where the similarity ended. Kevin was always getting into trouble, moving with the wrong crowd. Dad would watch us play football and warn me off him. I told Dad that even I knew to keep Kev at arm's length. In our last year at school there was a fight in the dining hall, and the male teachers attempting to restore order were attacked by Rawlings who smashed a chair over their heads. Shortly after there was a terrible bike crash. Kevin, the pillion passenger, was flung from the machine, smashing his arm against a lamp post. With his arm paralysed in a sling, we sat in the hall taking our O levels. He was a clever lad and would have breezed them. I watched a teacher pin his paper with drawing pins to the desk. He scribbled a few lines then stormed out. I never saw him again.

Six months later I entered Delta Wing. In the foyer was a wing cleaner, pushing a mop around. I instantly recognised him as Kevin Rawlings, now minus an arm. He looked up.

"Morning, guv," and continued mopping.

"Kevin, it's me," removing my peaked cap. He stared in disbelief. When he got over the shock we shook hands. He told me that he had been sentenced to sixteen years after meeting Ronnie Biggs in Rio and becoming friends.

"There by the grace of God, Tom, our paths could have been so different."

As I left the wing, he asked me if I would have to report our friendship. I said that I would but not to worry, we were not on the same wing so he wouldn't be moved.

"Good, I've only just got here."

Two weeks later he was shipped out.

HIV and AIDS

Back on Fraggle Rock, lunch over, it's Friday afternoon. No work because it's canteen, where prisoners get to spend their wages on food, soft drinks and tobacco. Earnings at that time were from £2 for the unemployed to £10 per week for a kitchen worker. The prison currency that is tobacco will be replaced by phone cards as more of the Woolf report recommendations are introduced (the maintenance of family ties via card phones). The domestic afternoon is busy with chapel, gym, library, exercise and canteen – there is mass movement of prisoners. Debts are settled and made; it can often be a dangerous afternoon.

Rushing around trying to get a bite to eat and air my gym kit before unlock, I was aware that some kind of special briefing was about to start due to the unusual presence of the wing governor and PO Jim. Two young men, both cat A's, had been located on the twos during lunch – Alfrey and Cassidy. They were "twentyish" the gov told us. He was struggling for the right words. SO Tony helped him out.
"They are both HIV positive. They have got AIDS," he said very directly. The older officers reacted instantly; this is what the gov had feared.
"We will refuse to unlock, get the POA down here," was said by Officer Ron who had plenty of support. Tony attempted to calm everyone down.
"We've got no choice. The number one governor has instructed us to take them."
The wing gov and PO Jim were nodding in agreement. Officer Ron, who had clearly taken on the role of spokesman, said, "The cons won't stand for it, they will be assaulted or worse."
We knew worse meant murder.
He added sarcastically, "Unless they are built like the 'Barnsley Beast' next door," referring to Reg Chapman, a rapist who could certainly handle himself and survive on normal location.

54

Tony was stuck between what he saw as doing right by his officers and the demands of senior management. Exasperated, he said, "Tom, go and get Stan."

As I made my way up the concrete wing stairs, I thought, "Bloody hell, not again. Who's running this prison?" Unlocking him, he was laying stretched out on his bed in his usual attire of Adidas Sambas, shorts and a new South African rugby top.

"Now what? Why aren't we unlocked?"

"You're wanted downstairs by the wing gov and PO," I replied, not wanting to give too much away for fear of the landing listening in. As we walked along the spur a few doors were kicked and a con shouted, "When are we fucking getting unlocked?" Stan threw me a look.

"This had better not take long, it's Friday afternoon, the lads are restless."

Stan walked straight into the office.

"What, Tone?" he said, ignoring everyone else, particularly the wing gov and PO Jim. SO Tony explained the situation. Stan said that the landing knew they had been brought on at lunchtime.

When Tony expanded, Stan replied, "They won't last the afternoon, what the fuck do you expect me to do?"

Officers began to mutter in agreement with the cat A's sentiments. Tony and Stan turned to the wing governor looking for answers. They were not forthcoming.

"You're keeping them and that's final," he said, pushing his way between the protesting officers and leaving the wing.

Stan then said, "I'll do my best, Tone, but there is going to be murders this afternoon."

Unlocking, with us all on high alert, I caught sight of our two new guests. They looked extremely young, vulnerable and nervous, other prisoners viewing them with suspicion. They couldn't have looked more out of their depth if they tried. The afternoon wore on and things appeared more relaxed. We made our way to the ones to supervise serving of tea. The hotplate was a similar affair to that of any motorway services, where prisoners would queue up to be served by other prisoners or hotplate orderlies. We just didn't have a till at the end. The food was good at Lartin, much of it prepared and cooked on the premises by prisoners. Madman Charlie Bronson says in his book *The Good Prison Guide*, "I will give Long Lartin 7/10. It does a lovely beef curry." With tea almost over, I heard the shrill of an alarm bell ring from upstairs. Instantly I knew where to run. On entering the twos landing, there was smoke everywhere. A hose reel was being deployed by Officer Ron. Officers Paul and Mark were down the spur, they were holding onto the two new receptions Alfrey and Cassidy. Their cells were ablaze. I think Officer Ron took great delight in extinguishing the fires with gallons of water that he sprayed everywhere. More staff arrived and the landing was evacuated due to the deadly smoke that clung everywhere. The two victims of arson were removed to the seg unit for their own protection. Luckily for them it was only their property that had gone up in smoke.

Christmas Cake

Having been on Foxy for almost four years now I was looking to move on. Confident in my abilities, I had been interested in working in Long Lartin's segregation unit for some time. Call it what you will, the seg, block, chokey, or if you were in a Victorian jail the dungeon. It wasn't for everyone and SO Tony was encouraging and supportive of my application. Cat A prisoner Stan was not.

"What on earth do you want to go down the chokey for? He wants to bash us up, Del."

Del, pragmatic as ever, simply said, "Take no notice, Tom, you'll be fine."

I received a letter from our training unit sending me on a two-week course to Wakefield. The letter informed me that the training was for the ECR. That was the last place I wanted to work. The control room, night shifts every six weeks – no thank you. Worse still, if I completed the course I would surely be moved. Then I bumped into Officer Taff. We had the same surname and more importantly he wanted to go to the ECR. Our mail was always being muddled up, I even got Paddy Hill's mail on a couple of occasions, an IRA Birmingham pub bomber, one of the six. So, the envelope was simply handed over to Taff and it worked. He completed the course and moved into the ECR a couple of months later, no questions asked. I was off to the chokey after Christmas.

Christmas at Lartin wasn't too bad as far as Christmas goes in prison. Each wing had a tree and lights and decorations were very imaginative and creative. On occasions, the crowning piece on top of the tree would cause discussion, particularly when it had the number one governor or some infamous prisoner's face on it. Some prisoners really went to town with the decoration of their cells, others didn't bother, it was just another day to them. Officer Charlie was always a larger-than-life Father Christmas. He would make appearances at the staff social club, the visits hall, and on the big day he would welcome us in for the morning shift and then wander around the wings. It lifted everyone's spirits. The children of the prisoners and staff loved him. Pool, darts, table tennis and quiz competitions were fiercely competitive. Staff would join in; it broke down barriers. One year Officer Mark arrived from Preston. He was a county table tennis champion so the cons got a shock that year. There would be tension in the run up to the festive season and hooch brewing would go into overdrive, so we had to ensure that we found at least some of it, maintaining a balance.

My last Christmas Day went well until teatime. The trolley arrived onto the wing full of the usual Christmas fare until some bright spark pointed out that the Christmas cake was missing. With home time rapidly approaching, I went off to the kitchen to track it down. A beautiful homemade cake was handed to me by a prisoner. It even had Foxy Wing iced on the top. "I did that," he announced proudly.
"Nice one."
I delivered it to the wing displaying it on a table by the hotplate, when out of nowhere cat A Eric Von-Bulow (cop killer) stole it. Running upstairs, I gave chase. Catching him at his cell, I wrestled the cake off him. It was a Keystone Cops moment. Back downstairs I was loudly applauded by the cons and officers. SO Tony came to see what the commotion was about. I explained. He told me to "nick him" for it. "Come on, Tone, it's Christmas and I want to go home."
In front of the staff and prisoners, he put me in my place.
"You're not down the block yet, I'm still your boss. Got it?"
"Yes, Tone," I said, much to the amusement of everyone.

Segregation Unit

I knew a few of the lads down the seg unit. It wasn't actually "down" anywhere, it's just another prison expression. In Victorian jails they were often down steep steps, the dungeons, Wandsworth being a classic example. I had been there on escort taking one of our cons on transfer for accumulated visits (A/V's). A prisoner could save up his visiting orders (V/O's) then apply to have his visits at a jail nearer home, usually a local jail. We would move him there for a month. Often the prisoner would return to us complaining how limited the regime was:

"Loads of bang up, guv."

"I got to see my old mum, she's not so good on her feet now."

"The grub's crap."

"The screws don't talk to you."

These were all common quotes of their holiday experience.

On arrival at Wandsworth's infamous seg unit, we descended down a long flight of steep steps from the main prison. The unit screws were all giants. Immediately after the cuffs had been removed by us they surrounded him, giving the prisoner instructions to strip, face the wall then squat. His clothes were kicked aside and he was then ordered into a cell, still naked. Prison issue kit inside.

"Welcome to Wandsworth, happiness is door shaped," said the screw slamming the door firmly shut.

Our SO explained that the con was only there for A/V's, he hadn't assaulted anyone.

"He'd know it if he had. This is our block, he will be upstairs tomorrow. Why don't you lot fuck off to our Mess before you go home?"

The SO didn't reply. We went off in search of the Mess. Best not ask them for directions we figured.

First shift in the block. I was apprehensive not wanting to let anyone down. It's like a prison within a prison – fully self-contained; two floors, eighteen cells on the ground floor, ten cells upstairs, plus two strip cells or boxes. A self-contained exercise yard within the block. The strip cells are two reinforced concrete cells with a six-inch raised concrete plinth for a bed. The prisoner who entered them would be stripped of clothes, jewellery and given an anti-ligature blanket, shorts and top. There would be a cardboard "pisspot" included, that was literally it. They were secured by a double door system for added security but mostly to restrict noise. Those who occupied "special accommodation", the official name on the form, would be subject to a regular special watch. A governor grade would be required to sanction their ongoing use once a prisoner was located. They were used by offenders who had become completely non-compliant and refractory, often after assaulting a member of staff or another prisoner. It was to maintain safety for all, a time to cool off and calm down. We also used them for self-harmers and those at risk of suicide, however, this was beginning to be questioned as to whether these were appropriate reasons for their use. A body belt was another tool used to control the individual within the box. As the name suggests, this was a heavy, wide leather belt secured at the base of the spine by a padlock. At the side of the belt were two manacles to secure the wrists and therefore immobilise the prisoner. This may sound inhumane or barbaric to some readers, but it is difficult to comprehend the level of violence some prisoners are capable of. It always, even after thirty-two years of service, shocked me what one human can afflict on another.

The front six cells directly opposite the office were holding cells. Prisoners would be assessed as to their behaviour and compliance before being moved around the back to cells with a metal sink and toilet. The first task of the shift was to "slop out" these cells one at a time. First day, first hour, second cell. The prisoner stepped out, picked up a metal mop bucket and proceeded to smash the porcelain overhead toilet system and anything else breakable in the recess. Water flowing everywhere, I pressed the alarm bell and joined my new colleagues in restraining him. After he had launched the bucket through the office window at the SO he was placed in "special accommodation". SO Gordon, a straight-talking Scotsman who I struggled to understand, my new boss, called us into the office. Doors were now being banged around the block; the noise was deafening as well as frightening. Prisoners were screaming threats of revenge towards us, in some sort of twisted support of the prisoner in the box.

"Okay, tea and toast, Hilly, then we will move at our pace. Oh yeah, Tom, we don't press the bell down here unless we really have to."

"Yes, boss. Got it," I replied feeling pretty small now.

"You did good though," he said smiling and shouting above the din from the cons. I instantly felt part of the team from that simple smile and comment with me passing around the brews to my new teammates.

Downstairs we housed those held on Prison Rule 43 G.O.A.D. Translated, that meant prisoners held in segregation or solitary for the Good Order and Discipline of the establishment. The mad, bad and dangerous. Also, those on Rule 47 pending a disciplinary award. Adjudications for prisoners placed on governor's report would be held in the unit Monday to Saturday. A governor would listen and adjudicate the charge. The setting for this was like a mini court. The accused would be marched in, give his name and number to the governor, then seated with an officer in close attendance either side. The charge read out, these often very serious charges, would sometimes decline into hilarious farces with prisoners defending themselves as if they were back in the Old Bailey and their lives literally depending on the outcome. Written supporting evidence was presented and witnesses called. The service was doing its level best to appear fair and transparent.

Upstairs, the prisoners were under protection (Rule 43P). At this time, Long Lartin did not hold many sex offenders and there was no vulnerable prisoners wing (VP's Wing). Some of these residents were in extreme debt to other prisoners in the main prison or their crime made it impossible to exist on normal location. For example, the evil Michael Sams who

61

kidnapped and later murdered Julie Dart in 1991. He subsequently kidnapped Stephanie Slater in 1992, an estate agent who he met "viewing" a property. She was eventually released after the payment of a ransom. I remember buying a house in Evesham in the early nineties. An unaccompanied female estate agent took me inside for the viewing and I simply couldn't get that monster Sams out of my head. I did buy the house though.

Simon Bowman Part 1

The unit's doors swung open and a young man who had a striking resemblance to "Desperate Dan" was escorted in surrounded by officers. He wasn't happy, ranting about how he wouldn't do any more time other than his original sentence. He then focused his attention on us.

"Don't think you lot will be able to control me either," he raged in a Geordie accent. What was his problem? I thought. After a tension filled strip search, which every prisoner would have upon entering the unit, we would find out. The escort told us that the uncooperative and threatening Geordie was Simon Bowman. He had escaped from Durham jail.

"The first person to do so since McVicar," one of the escorts said proudly.

That would be John McVicar he was referring to who had indeed escaped in 1968 and had been immortalised in the film of the same name played by The Who's front man, Roger Daltrey in 1980. I was familiar with this story. They had escaped from Durham's special secure unit, even using John Straffen to move bricks and mortar for them in his tea urns. McVicar's son was held at Long Lartin, charged under an alias, Russell Grant. He would keep a low profile. Bowman had been convicted of conspiracy to commit armed robbery and was sentenced to twelve years. There had been a manhunt, eventually tracking him down to the southeast of England. Armed police had surrounded a terrace of houses where they believed him to be. Yet again he gave them the slip, actually knocking over a cop as he fled across fields pursued by dogs. After swimming across a river, he was eventually recaptured. There would now be a trial for the escape and firearm offences committed during his bid for freedom. He was to be held by us until the judiciary were ready for his return to the north. The escort departed.

"Good luck, boys, you'll need it. He's fucking dangerous and off his nut."

We took stock and unlocked him for what we hoped would be a productive chat. When he was reasonably calm between

63

outbursts against most authority, in particular the police, he told us he was concerned that any court in the northeast would lock him up and throw away the key. His main concern being the firearm offence against him whilst evading capture by the police. The escape charge he accepted.

"I'm not going to do life for no fucker. This is the bizzies chance to get me off the street for good."

Then it was onto the usual demands:

"Where's me prop?"

"I need to phone my brief."

"I want a shower."

And so forth...

There was an underlying current of aggression throughout. When we locked him back up I was relieved it was my long weekend off.

Meanwhile – Back in the Seg

There is a strict regime in any block, but this is always disrupted by incidents that occur in the main prison or in the block itself. As soon as the alarm bell sounded anywhere in the establishment, we would stop everything, secure the unit, open the double doors, unlock a holding cell and strip box. All this whilst waiting to be informed by the control room of one of the following three scenarios:

One on the way under restraint.

One on the way walking.

Alarm bell false.

Of course, we had our own population to deal with, the most disruptive and aggressive in the entire prison system. Segregation in a maximum security cat A dispersal prison. They would do their best on a daily basis to live up to that reputation.

So many passed through our doors, often for short periods on "twenty-eight day lie downs" from another dispersal. They were on the "ghost train", "the merry go-round", "the circuit". "Shipped" or "ghosted" from one seg unit to another, allowing everyone a break. The trouble was you never knew who or what you would get in return. One lad, and I'm sorry I don't remember his name, would be constantly working out in his cell – mainly press-ups. He had been in the army. When we unlocked him he would stand rigid to attention, drenched in sweat. It was like he had walked out of a swimming pool fully clothed in his maroon prison issue tracksuit. He loved nothing more than to jump us without warning. This meant a roll around, then him in the box. Within an hour we would allow him back to his cell, completely calm now. We would be congratulated on our performance or lack of it in his own restraint with him often complaining that we hadn't used a body belt. He kept us on our toes but we all liked him. Looking back, he was clearly ill. Really sad but really dangerous. Imagine bumping into him on a Saturday night out fuelled with drink and drugs. Your worst nightmare.

Others included Lee Cooper (murder). He handed me his daily application one morning. I hadn't looked up, accepting the form indicating if he was requesting a shower, a book, the chaplain, the doctor etc, when I noted a message written across it: "I have the right to remain silent". Puzzled, looking up, Cooper had managed to sew his lips shut with green thread he had unpicked from his prison blanket, the wool hanging from the corner of his lips. The stitches looked like Frankenstein. Bizarre doesn't even begin to cover it. He was marched off to the hospital.

A prisoner who had officially changed his name to "Girl" (the prison service allowed this) would parade out of his cell dressed in short shorts complete with pink mule slippers and a blonde bob-style wig. The other cons called him Myra as in Myra Hindley. Later on in Bravo Wing we would have a Marcia and Mary, all very confusing and very dangerous. There was even a "Sir". He had gone to extreme lengths to change his name by deed poll in order that we, the service, would address him as "Sir". He would storm to the office complaining whenever he was called as we would deliberately request the presence of Prisoner AB1214 to the wing office.

Jeremy Bamber

New staff were replacing colleagues who had done their time in the unit, usually between two and four years. Some dealt with the added pressures of the environment better than others. Officers who had arrived just after me post-"Fresh Start" were filtering in. Officer Psycho Davies was a welcome addition. To say that he brought something different to the party was an understatement, yet despite his eccentricities he was level-headed and cool under pressure. (Did I just say that?) SO Terry came to us from HMP Stafford. Right away we knew he was a positive addition, even if he did insist on wearing a couple of bin bags "to sweat it out, Tom" during teatime five-a-side football. We were a tight crew now, socialising and playing sport together, our wives and girlfriends also bonding in the group.

Jeremy Bamber became our latest guest to arrive. He was convicted of the 1985 White House Farm murders in Essex. Bamber's victims included his adoptive parents, Nevill and June Bamber, his sister Sheila Caffell and her six year old twin sons. Returning a majority verdict, the jury found that, after committing the murders in order to secure a large inheritance, Bamber had placed a rifle in the hands of his murdered twenty-eight year old sister who had been diagnosed with schizophrenia, to make the scene appear as if she had committed the murders and subsequent suicide. He is serving life imprisonment under a whole life tariff. He has repeatedly applied to have his conviction overturned or the life tariff removed. His extended family remain convinced of his guilt.

Jeremy Bamber is my age so we talked at length on occasions. He came across as both charming and patronising to many. Officer Fred would describe him as "a good con man". We all agreed. The more he tried to persuade me of his innocence, the more I felt he was as guilty as charged. We all did. There were too many holes in his version of the case. He once showed me some photographs of his girlfriend who visited him at the jail.

He had women writing to him from all over the country. He said his girlfriend was staying at The King Edward pub for the weekend, close to the jail. He suggested I visit her in the evening to play pool.

"I don't think so, Jeremy."

"You like pool, don't you? And I am sure you will like her," he replied with a knowing smile.

An example of how manipulative he could be. That evening I cycled past The King Edward on my route home and could see the pool table, laughing to myself as I cycled on.

My god-daughter, who was eight years old at the time, was badly burnt on her back when her pyjamas caught fire whilst she was warming herself by an electric fire. I was devastated. I mentioned it to Bamber who promptly went into action at the sewing and knitting group that bizarrely was held around the large governor's adjudication table in the unit. He presented me with a teddy bear of the highest quality that he had made for Gemma. I thanked him, gave it to her and we called it Bamber Bear.

Vincent Hickey

Between the ongoing daily chaos of us being assaulted, fires, floods, smash ups, dirty protests, fights, self-harm and suicide, Vincent Hickey turned up. He had only been back with us for a couple of days, located in a holding cell. It was the end of the evening duty shift before the arrival of night staff. We would place a flask of hot water in each cell, allowing them to make a last brew. Secure the cell door. Slide the bolt over. Final lock up. Unlocking Hickey's door to do this with Officer Mick, I placed the flask inside on the floor. The cell was in total darkness and silent. Something wasn't right. I switched the light on. Vincent Hickey was sat on the bed, slumped in a corner. There was blood everywhere, floor, walls and bed. He was barely conscious and very pale. All colour had drained out of him. There was a plastic biro pen rammed in on the inside of his arm at the elbow. Entering the cell always "shooting the lock" to prevent a hostage incident, Officer Mick went to grab Vinney, but much to his surprise I pushed him aside.

"Let me try talking to him first. Get me a towel."

Vinney looked up struggling to focus.

"Leave me, let me go."

I said that wasn't going to happen. We would get him medical attention.

Mick arrived with a towel and a couple of staff.

"No one cares, Tom, it doesn't matter anymore."

I said that I cared and it did matter.

"I was with you for that week of your appeal, Vinney, and I know that you are innocent, so do lots of others. Let me put the towel around your arm and we will get it looked at."

Thankfully, he finally agreed and we got him treated.

The following day SO Terry and I went to see him in the prison hospital. He was in much better spirits, apologising and thanking me for my actions the previous evening. Terry told him that we had to complete some new paperwork, proudly producing the new "Assessment, Care in Custody and

Teamwork" document (ACCT). It was an orange book full of new complex-looking forms replacing the single sheet "Self-Harm" form.

"Fuck me, I promise I won't do it again if you have to fill that lot in every time."

Simon Bowman Part 2

Arriving for my late shift at 12.30pm on a Tuesday afternoon after a long weekend off, I noticed cat A CF0558 Bowman on the roll board.

"Bloody hell, not him again," I said to staff having lunch in the office.

Officers Lenny and Fred both laughed and explained that he had arrived Friday evening and was fine now. Apparently, the firearm charges had been thrown out. He only had an extra two years added to the original twelve years for the escape.

"Moving him around the back this afternoon," said Lenny in between eating a sandwich and polishing his boots.

Fred chipped in, "Yeah, we may give him the job as seg cleaner. Different person, Tom."

"WHAT?"

I couldn't believe what I was hearing. Sure enough, after lunch we unlocked the new Simon Bowman. It was as if he had had a personality transplant. Polite, charming, funny and helpful. Happy to be out of the northeast with us. Within a fortnight he was indeed the unit's trusted cleaner. Transformation complete.

Taxi

Category B escorts were taken in taxis as opposed to the cat A's in special cellular vehicles. Steve Selby Taxis had the contract for this operation. He also happened to be the Mayor of Evesham. Steve was an asset to the service and I would always tell him how much better his security briefings were than the actual security department at Long Lartin, much to their annoyance. If you were going to outside hospital or court, he would brief you on all manner of things with up to the minute information – what ward the prisoner was located, what was wrong with him, how he was behaving, who the staff you were relieving were, right down to the menu in the hospital canteen. The same detail was relayed for courts and even funeral escorts. His only downside was the actual driving experience. He thought he was above the law driving for the service and therefore exempt from all national speed limits. He was often told to slow down by the staff or prisoner. At least he always knew the route. The same could not be said for Skippy Jones, one of his two drivers, the other being Steve's wife who was the best of the three, a very competent and level-headed woman. Skippy on the other hand, an ex principal officer, who had transferred from the Australian prison service to ours and had now retired, had no idea where anywhere was in the country and drove like Miss Daisy.

A Grand Day Out

The prison service had begun to lose its way after the riots and the resulting Woolf report. Prisoners had somehow become empowered and were now exploiting that power. Incredibly, the service was giving in to the demands of convicted prisoners. Simon Bowman had settled into his role as the segregation unit's trusted orderly. He was granted many perks that would seem unreal before or after that time in the early to mid-nineties. For example, a video recorder appeared. One evening the staff watched his copy of *The Godfather* that he had had posted in. He then announced that he may be travelling to Newcastle for the day.

"For a court hearing?" I said.

"No, man. For a day out to see my dying dad. I've applied to the governor and it's being considered," he said, adding that if granted it would be under the terms of a day release licence, escorted by a single officer.

"No cuffs. In a taxi. You and me on a day trip to Newcastle. Fancy it, Tom? I've got to name an officer."

This was how lax things were becoming. A serving category A prisoner being held in a maximum security segregation unit with many years left on his sentence being allowed out for "a day trip". Not to mention his escape history. Despite our protests and reservations the Home Office approved his application. It was on and I was going with him. Once I established that no blame or responsibility would fall on me when he simply absconded at the earliest opportunity, I began to relax. Simon did promise that he would not simply walk off at the first services. He valued the trust that had been given by the service, viewing it as a chance to earn early parole. He also promised to not let me down. All very reassuring – not.

Preparation for the "grand day out" was in full swing. This involved Simon having his "flat top" hairstyle freshly cut by the prison barber (a con) who was paid £1 per haircut by the prison. I had mine done too. Then we discussed what we would wear as well as the itinerary. It was becoming clear that Bowman's father was not as ill as the Home Office was led to believe. I collected the licence from the governing governor's secretary, checking the details. It would allow us out of the jail at 6am and we had to be back by 9pm.

I arrived at the gate at 5am and drew my keys. I then began to make my way to the block, full of trepidation as to how the day would go. I unlocked Simon, who was ready to go. We walked out of the jail to rather bemused night staff. These were unusual times. Waiting for us outside was the Mayor of Evesham, Steve, sat in his Vauxhall Carlton taxi. We jumped in and sped off to Newcastle. Once on the motorway Steve didn't drop below 100mph to Simon's approval. We stopped at a services for the loo. This is it, I thought to myself.

On returning to the taxi I could see Steve eyeing me in his rear-view mirror. As I slid in he looked at me anxiously.
"What do you reckon?"
I replied that we should wait a few minutes before calling it in. In the distance, Steve spotted him.
"There he is," he exclaimed excitedly.
Sure enough there was Bowman bouncing toward us, his hands full of pop and snacks.
"There you go. Now just relax and we can have a great day. I could have made off in any of those lorries," indicating the huge lorry park. "I wouldn't do that to you, Tom."
Steve smiled at me in agreement as we shot forward on our journey. Simon passed a cassette tape to Steve.
"Put that on, guv, and play it loud."
Steve obliged. Then, one of the most surreal moments ever. Booming out of the car stereo system, just as in the scene from the film *McVicar*, "Free me" by Roger Daltrey, the three of us laughing, singing along, racing up the M1.

On arrival in a city I had never been to before we pulled up at his dad's address. Steve had agreed to leave us to it as he was going to have a sleep before the return journey. Simon's dad, as I had expected, was in fine health. We had a cuppa and after half an hour Simon told him that we were off out. We would call back before we headed south, back to jail. His dad handed him a set of keys and a wad of cash. "Have fun, lads, see you later," he said, waving us off. Simon unlocked a garage under the house and revealed a Ford Mondeo.

"Who's is that? Have you still got a licence? Where are we going?" were just some of my questions to him as we left for the centre of town.

"Have you got your ID card?" Before I could reply, he added, "Don't be flashing it to the bizzies if we get pulled, just keep your hands out and do as they say. They will fucking shoot us and ask questions later."

He wasn't joking. The reality was all too apparent as he pointed out post offices, jewellery shops and building societies that he had "turned over" without being caught.

"Ironic really, I get banged up for twelve and I haven't actually carried out the job, just got grassed up by my girlfriend."

Months later I discovered that the girlfriend had had her house burnt out whilst Simon was banged up. Very conveniently for him.

After the guided tour of armed robberies, it was off to visit his pal in South Shields. "Don't say nothing and you're definitely not a screw."

"Yeah, yeah."

I was getting accustomed to being undercover. His mate was understandably shocked when he opened the door.

"Fuck, Simon, have you escaped again? You on the run?"

Bowman simply brushed these comments aside, introducing me as beers were produced. When I spoke, shock reappeared on his face due to my Bristolian accent. Simon was in his element now.

"He's my pal from down south, we are doing a job down there. A good earner. Anyhow, nice to see you, we better get off before the bizzies turn up unannounced." The tension was building. I was imagining armed police surrounding the house any second and so was Simon's pal, as he quickly ushered us on our way. Back in the car now, it was off for a spot of lunch and a few bevvies in a posh hotel.

"My old man is picking up the bill," Simon stated. There we were sitting in a lovely hotel looking out at the North Sea enjoying lunch when Simon spots two girls. I didn't need any encouragement, feeling relaxed after a few drinks. We made our move with Simon ordering champagne for our party. One of the girls was a waitress and worked at the hotel. The other was, unbelievably, a policewoman who had only recently completed her training. We both found this hilarious. Simon was testing her knowledge of the chief constable and other high-ranking cops in Northumbria police force, whilst I was displaying the licence and my ID card on the table. I don't think they really believed it. An armed robber and a prison officer on a grand day out.

Driving back to Simon's dad, a quick exchange of goodbyes and we sped off with Steve driving again at breakneck speed, heading south. Arriving close to the jail at around 8pm, the three of us decided we still had time for a nightcap. The mayor, the armed robber and the prison officer all had a pint before we arrived back at the big house.

Simon thanked Steve for his speedy driving. I escorted him back to his cell, thanking him for a great, if not surreal, day out. He told me that he had demonstrated to the Home Office he should come "off the book", an expression meaning to be down categorised from cat A to cat B. I agreed with him. Privately I felt, although he had returned to prison, he had not demonstrated any reduction in his risk to the public or police. Quite the opposite, he was still a dangerous individual.

Changes

In September 1994 six exceptional risk category A prisoners escaped from HMP Whitemoor, Special Secure Unit (SSU), Cambridgeshire. Five were IRA, the other, Andy Russell, who featured in *Helicopters* and *Riot and Attempted Escape*. A gun had been used, several shots were fired and a prison officer was wounded. All six were recaptured within a couple of hours in the Fenlands surrounding the prison.

On 3 January 1995, two category A prisoners and one category B escaped from HMP Parkhurst on the Isle of Wight. They were recaptured on 8 January. A firearm and ammunition were present.

These escapes led to the Learmont and Woodcock enquires and subsequent reports, led by General Sir John Learmont and Sir John Woodcock. They were both comprehensive and authoritative whilst making serious criticisms of the prison service. The Learmont report stated, "Alarm Bells should have been ringing throughout the prison service." They were now. The service was about to change for the better as a direct result of this report and their recommendations.

Parkhurst was taken out of the dispersal system immediately, losing its category A status. The phrase "prison conditions should be decent but austere" had great importance attached to it. Maximum security jails had the spotlight on them in particular as they had become so lax in their security and regimes, evidenced by the high-profile escapes. The media had a field day. There were headlines in the papers every day that highlighted how bad things had become in dispersals. Then it was our turn.

Long Lartin had gone into lockdown, a full standdown search underway. Unlike Whitemoor at least, the explosive Semtex wasn't discovered. What was found though, was disturbing – homemade weapons of all descriptions, hooch, brewing equipment, drugs, drug paraphernalia, cash and escape equipment. What was equally shocking was the amount of it. We were shown the display. It was all laid on three very long trestle tables in the training unit. Simply staggering. You could not squeeze another illicit article on the tables. A double page photograph of the tables and their contents somehow made it into *The Sun* newspaper.

The majority of staff, including myself, were keen to implement the report's recommendations at once. There was a hesitancy from the senior management team at Lartin to make all the changes in one go. In hindsight this was the correct decision. There was a gradual change of rules and policy brought about during the following six months.

Prisoners' property was first on the agenda. Every con would be required to fit everything into two boxes to be stored under their bed. This was known as volumetric control. Excess kit was removed to reception. There was a lot of it. Suddenly, cells were sparse and landings clear as it should be. This in turn allowed for ease of searching cells and areas. It transformed wings into becoming clean and orderly.

Payphones were installed, one on each landing with phonecard operation that the prisoner purchased. No more use of official phones in offices by prisoners.

The prison canteen purchase list was rewritten. Only items on the official list could be purchased. No more purchasing items from local supermarkets by prison staff. Suddenly, salmon, steak and lobster were off the menu. Prisoners were no longer to be paid in cash. Now it was credit spend accounts. Jails that had allowed ice cream vans in (not Long Lartin) were prohibited. At Whitemoor they had even discovered a mountain bike that a prisoner had been allowed to purchase and ride around their association field.

The best was left until last. Prisoners were now to earn privileges. A national framework of incentives and earned privileges was introduced (IEP). It was to encourage good behaviour. There were three levels by which a prisoner's behaviour and attitude toward his offence (remorse or admission of guilt) would be graded. Basic, standard and enhanced level. Those who were identified as basic level prisoners would be removed from their wing to a newly identified Basic Wing. In our case F Wing. Staff volunteered and were selected to work there. Prisoners would remain there for twenty-eight days under a strict basic regime. No TV. Prison clothes only. No cooking facilities. No work. There was limited association and exercise periods with their wing only. It worked. By the removal of non-conformist, often awkward but not necessarily violent individuals to the Basic Wing, the remaining residential units became far more stable and better places to both work and live.

Simon Bowman Part 3 (The Finale)

Overnight our jail became a safer environment for staff and prisoners alike. Suddenly there were no "grey areas". Any initiatives that had been questionable were immediately scrapped. As for the segregation unit, the same applied. The sewing and knitting class came to an abrupt end. Exercise periods were a strict one hour and now supervised. Prisoners' possessions were cut to a minimum. There was now no doubt who was in charge.

Simon Bowman reverted to type, resigning his job as the unit's cleaner due to his wages and privileges being slashed. He was now banged up behind his door twenty-three hours a day due to his refusal to work or relocate to F Wing basic for twenty-eight days. He asked to talk with me privately. We met in the interview room. Even the setting of our chat appeared to unsettle him. We discussed the regime changes and he felt that he would remain cat A and never progress. I had to agree with him. Like a bolt of lightning he said, "I've got to get out of here. Tom, will you help?"
"What are you talking about? Off the unit? Another jail?"
"No. Escape." It was clear he was serious.
"You're joking, right?"
"No. You and a couple of other lads on the unit can take me to outside hospital. Leave the rest to me. Money will be transferred into your accounts."
I made it clear that this would not happen and that I believed no staff on the unit would assist him. He stared directly at me.
"Are you going to report this?"
"Yes. There is nothing more to say, Simon."
"Then fucking bang me up."
I did just that. I went straight to the security department telling them everything about the conversation with Bowman, writing it down on a security information report (SIR). The security PO instructed me not to speak about this to any other staff saying that two other officers on the unit had already been

approached. Within the week he was gone, ghosted to HMP Full Sutton in York. We were all relieved.

Six months later, at home listening to the radio, the national news bulletin announced that a dangerous prisoner had escaped whilst being treated at the Royal Preston Hospital. The public were warned not to approach him. His name was Simon Bowman. Eventually, he was recaptured by the police.

Months later I received a letter at the jail from Bowman who was now held at HMP Whitemoor. He was asking me to be a character witness for him at the Old Bailey. He said, "I'm pleading guilty to escaping and an incident in a taxi when I was being arrested." Needless to say, I never replied.

Promotion

After completing almost four years in the segregation unit management were looking to move me on. Lads were moving off the unit to Foxtrot Basic Wing. This was viewed as a means to gradually reintegrate officers back to normal wings, proving we had almost become as conditioned and institutionalised as our charges. For me this was definitely true. I had no wish or desire to leave. One option open to me was the newly formed Dedicated Search Teams (DST). Their formation had come about as a recommendation from the Woodcock report. They came under the umbrella of security and reported directly to them. A small, close-knit team was appealing. Plus, the attraction of a smart new combat-style uniform. Ironic really, in the early nineties we had been encouraged to ditch our slashed peaked caps and bulled boots. Now it was all change. I was always amazed how one person at the top dictated a policy and it was followed, almost unquestionably, by senior managers and governors alike. I guess they were just chasing their next promotion.

Completing a fortnight course for DST, it was clear to me that I wasn't suited to the role. I have always felt that any security department took itself far too seriously, believing it was a branch of MI5. Ours was no exception. Now they even looked like the German Gestapo as well as acting like them.

Arriving back at the jail after the course, feeling a little deflated, I approached the deputy governor asking if I could remain another twelve months in the unit.
"I will come down there tomorrow, I may have an option you might be interested in." What on earth did that mean? The following day the dep arrived at 10am sharp for adjudications, indicating he would speak with me after the "nickings". Sitting at the adjudication table with a picture of the Queen hanging behind him he said, "How do you fancy becoming an acting senior officer?"

Stunned, I replied, "Where? I haven't even taken the promotional exam."

He laughed telling me that it would be in situ. The block and I had better book myself a place on the promotion classes.

"You are the most experienced and best suited officer on the unit for the job."

I wasn't so sure. How would the boys react? Especially Officer Lenny who I knew was seeking promotion. The gov sensed my thoughts.

"It's up to you, we weren't sure if you would take it."

My mind was made up.

"Yes, I'll take it. Thank you."

The deputy governor stood up, shook my hand and congratulated me.

"You start tomorrow."

The very next morning, in my new role as Acting Senior Officer of HMP Long Lartin Segregation Unit, I headed over to the administration block to see Administration Officer (A.O.) Matt. He told me he would help input the officers' hours, overtime etc into the computer and show me how to produce a weekly detailed roster.

"Bring it all over, Tom, we will fly through it."

I knew it wasn't that simple. This was the civil service and my computer skills were very limited. I had left a very capable Officer Lenny in charge (IC). On my return to the unit carrying bundles of folders and paperwork, my head spinning with fresh ideas, I unlocked the double doors. The scene that greeted me was chaotic. Hose reels strewn over the floor, water everywhere, smoke hanging from the ceilings. Officer Lenny approached reporting, "Two cell fires, one con in the box, one con upstairs being treated for smoke inhalation. Oh, and the governor has phoned. Bronson is being moved down at lunchtime," he added matter-of-factly.

"Thanks, Lenny."

"No probs, Tom, bet you won't be going to admin again in a hurry with that lot," he said indicating to the paperwork.

"No, I won't leave the unit again. Admin will have to come to us."

We both laughed and discussed how we would deal with Charlie Bronson.

Mad World

Bizarrely, another prisoner had accused Bronson of rape, an accusation of course that he rebuked. All we were concerned about was where did they plan on relocating the alleged victim? Sense prevailed and he was moved to the hospital for his own protection with a view to ship him out ASAP. Bronson duly arrived on the block escorted by a C&R team in full kit. He was fully compliant despite the accusations against him. The team departed taking their gear with them.

"Good luck," they said slamming the doors behind them. I gathered the lads into the office for a quick pep talk, feeling the weight of responsibility fully on my shoulders. What would SO Tony or Terry say or do? This line of thought would often come into my head over the remainder of my career.

"Charlie likes routine so let's do it on time, no fucking about. Stay close to each other. Remember, he likes to take hostages. Don't give him any opportunities."

We gathered at his door to unlock him for exercise. He would be exercised alone. All eyes on me, I drew my keys and cautiously unlocked the door, pushing it open. Bronson leapt to attention, standing in the doorframe, staring directly ahead.

"One hour exercise period, Charlie."

He immediately marched out of the cell towards the gate to the yard. It was comical but thankfully no one laughed. I was happy that he hadn't entered into conversation with us. Within seconds of him striding across the yard cell buzzers went off around the unit. Other prisoners wanted to join him on exercise. They were all yelling their support for him. There was also talk of serious revenge being handed out to the con who dared level such accusations at Bronson. Charlie lapped it up. He was also acknowledging his peers at their cell windows as if he were the king. In some mad way he was.

The week passed without incident, Bronson enjoying his stay with us, be it a regimented one. I got news that the alleged rape victim had been shipped out. Bronson would be allowed to return to normal location as he had demonstrated good behaviour with us. I relayed this information to him. He thanked me for a pleasant stay adding that justice had prevailed. It was Sunday afternoon and he went straight out to the association field. Standing on the football pitch centre circle, interrupting a match that was in full flow, he proceeded to give a speech proclaiming his innocence.

"If any person, con or screw doubted it, they should say so now or forever hold their peace."

Total silence. Everyone stopped and turned towards Charlie. Applause broke out and shouts of support. He raised his hand walking off the pitch. Then the football resumed and the cons continued their association. All was well again in our mad world.

Back to School

Promotion classes were held weekly for two hours in the training unit. They started in March for the exam in June. The Prison Service Promotion Exam was similar to the sergeant's examination in the police force. It consisted of a prison technical paper and two five hundred-word essays; forty minutes were allowed apiece. Topics were prison related: "With the service under extreme pressure of overcrowding, what are its options?" Discuss. There were twenty-five officers in attendance for the first class including myself and officers Lenny and Fred. We knew only about twenty per cent would be successful. When we left that evening, our arms full of books and folders, with the homework essay to complete by the following week, it was very daunting. Officer Fred was questioning himself as to why he was even doing it. The next morning he told me that he had lost sleep over it. I suggested that if his heart wasn't in it maybe he should return everything to the training unit. At lunch time he was ecstatic, telling all he had taken my advice and he felt a giant weight had been lifted from his shoulders. He laughed adding, "You have no choice but to sit the exam."

Murder

David Amani and Richard Thompson were brought onto the unit. They had murdered a fellow prisoner at Long Lartin, a sex offender who was serving nine years. It later materialised that they had kicked him to death. The pair were to be held by us whilst the police and prison services carried out their respective investigations. Immediately the two prisoners went on "dirty protest". As time passed conditions worsened. Rapidly the stench became overwhelming. When we unlocked them one or two of us, including myself, were gagging. They had covered both themselves and their cells in excrement.

Cocooned in the office during lunch with the door firmly shut, I was attempting to revise and produce a detail for the following week. Officers Fred and Brian were playing cards and somehow eating lunch when the office door swung open. It was the number one governor with a gentleman whom I realised was the director general of the prison service – only by reading his name badge. Derek Lewis. Leaping up I gave the roll. Twenty-six including twelve cat A's, staring at my fellow officers who eventually stopped eating and stood up. I guessed correctly they had no idea who our guest was. They assumed he was just another suit from the Home Office. The DG asked if we could unlock a prisoner for a brief chat. Before I could answer, Officer Brian was unlocking David Amani's cell with the director general in tow. The total expression of horror across Derek Lewis's face was priceless. Amani, his face covered in shit just staring at him. I had to tell Brian to shut the door before he passed out with the awful smell. The number one governor said, "Thank you, Tom, I think we will continue our tour elsewhere," a wry smile spreading across his face. The DG was still struggling to recover his composure as he left the unit. I asked Brian what he was thinking, opening up a dirty protest for the director general. He replied he wasn't thinking. Fred and I fell about laughing. Brian shrugged his shoulders and finished his lunch.

A couple of weeks passed. I was instructed to take Dave Amani to HMP Wakefield. I would be IC of the escort. I had struck up some kind of rapport with Amani so I didn't foresee any potential issues with the transfer. A bonus was he was happy to be leaving Lartin, resulting in an end to the dirty protest.

Heading north there were no problems until we reached the outskirts of Nottingham. He had become highly agitated smashing his handcuffs against his cell, demanding we go to the nearest motorway services to allow him to use the toilet facilities. I told him that would not be happening. The cat A van navigator meanwhile had contacted a secure police station en route that could accommodate us. Arriving at a brand new, state of the art police station I was happy with my decision. There were half a dozen police officers and a dog handler all being directed by an inspector. Exiting the van Amani snarled at them. I cracked a joke with him to lower the tension. It worked and we started chatting as we were escorted into the station, the Old Bill taking a dim view that we even spoke to prisoners. The inspector opened the door to a tiny cubicle with a toilet and small sink, all brick built. Perfect. I took off his handcuffs and those securing him to an officer. The inspector closed the door. On his exit as I was reapplying the cuffs, grinning he said to the inspector and his officers, "I was going to have some fun with you lot, but out of respect of the boss," indicating me, "I didn't."

The inspector was puzzled.

Amani continued, "Look at the ceiling, it's false. I could have got up there on the cistern into the roof space and ripped it to bits."

In unison the police and prison officers all looked up. He was right, the police were fuming.

"Thanks, Dave, for not wrecking their new police station," I said.

We arrived at Wakefield without further incident.

Assault

Being assaulted was seen as part of the job description in any segregation unit. It shouldn't happen but it did. A lot of the lads actually preferred to be punched or spat at rather than being potted (having excrement thrown over you). Personally, I preferred the latter. A trip to the shower was far better than one to the dentist.

A new arrival who had assaulted an officer on the wings was causing us problems. Refusing to comply, he was being placed in and out of the box. I entered his cell with Officers Lenny and Brian. Laying on the floor he was refusing to engage. As we exited he sprang to his feet biting the inside of my right arm. Falling to the floor I couldn't get him to release his grip. I didn't want to pull my arm away as I felt his teeth sink further. Lenny drew his stave and struck him several times before he let go. He was restrained and moved to the box. I was treated by our healthcare staff who suggested I go to my doctor for blood tests. On arrival at the surgery in uniform, I told the receptionist that I had been bitten.
"Oh, by a dog?" she said.
"No, by a human," I replied. I was immediately taken to discuss this with the doctor who asked if I wanted counselling. I told her I didn't and that I was fine. The prison had just sent me for blood tests.
"That is what the counselling is for. To have the test or not."
Looking confused, she explained.
"In case the test for HIV comes back positive."
"Oh," I replied, a little dazed.
Two weeks later a negative test was confirmed. Thank goodness for that.

Recognition at last?

The Butler Trust Awards are for people working in a prison or probation setting. They are presented annually by HRH The Princess Royal at St James's Palace.

The segregation unit had been nominated as a collective by the board of visitors for our dedication and professionalism in dealing with some of the country's most dangerous and violent individuals. We felt honoured that someone was going to acknowledge our daily efforts officially.

The Recognition and Achievement Award was to be presented by the governing governor in the boardroom then on to the awards finale in London.

The lads on the unit packed themselves into Lartin's formal boardroom eagerly waiting the number one's arrival. I sat next to my opposite number, Senior Officer Derek, who had just arrived from HMP Whitemoor. As the governor entered we all stood to attention. He quickly motioned us to sit down. He made a great speech, bigging us up about our dedication, fortitude and resolve. Blah blah blah... Finally, he said, "It gives me great pleasure to present this award to the senior officer of the segregation unit."
All eyes were now on me as I felt myself rise from my chair to gladly accept our prize.
"Senior Officer Derek Hatton."
I sunk back down, embarrassed.
An equally surprised Derek, all six feet four, awkwardly got to his feet. The lads' shock quickly turned to laughter as an embarrassed Derek accepted our award.

Back on the unit Derek presented me with the trophy at a hastily arranged ceremony, with an equally hastily prepared speech.
"It gives me great pleasure to present this magnificent trophy to Acting Senior Officer Tom Hill."

We all fell about laughing as Substantive Senior Officer Derek extended his hand adding, "No hard feelings, mate, you deserve this more than me."

On Edge

There was one particular individual who really got to me during my time in the unit, a con we called Jacko. He was Polish, of slight build, mid-thirties and extremely unpredictable. Unlocking him "mob handed", we never knew who would appear. He could be fine and co-operative one day and the next he would launch himself at us with great dexterity and athleticism without warning, putting us all on edge for the remainder of the shift.

Climbing was one of his specialities. He should have been in the circus. During exercise he somehow managed to scale the inner wall of the yard and position himself astride the camera that watched over the area. I marched out ordering him to climb down before he fell to the concrete fifteen feet below. As he ignored my instructions the bracket became loose. Suddenly bracket, camera and Jacko fell to earth. We rushed him immediately but he had already sprung to his feet to meet us head on. Ten minutes later he would be back where he belonged, the box, with six exhausted screws enjoying a well-deserved brew.

Arriving one morning the night staff informed me that he had been placed in "special accommodation" during the night. After a sharp intake of breath from me they relayed their story. He had smashed up and flooded his cell in the early hours and demanded to be moved into the box to "straighten his head". I listened in disbelief. They continued with the story telling me how the night PO, who was now in hospital, in his wisdom had agreed to Jacko's request and unlocked the lunatic against the advice of his staff.

As they all descended the stone staircase from the upper landing with the elderly PO leading the way, Jacko had thrown himself down the stairs, attacking the PO in the process. Luckily there were some big lads on the night shift who after a long struggle managed to drag him away.

"He's not been stripped, Tom, we just about managed to get him in."

"Okay, leave it to the professionals," I joked.

After slop out and breakfast we turned our attention to Jacko who appeared quiet and calm, obeying instructions to face the back wall and place his hands on his head whilst kneeling. As the second steel door was swung open, without warning he leapt up rushing us with what appeared to be a shank. Quick thinking Officer Ian somehow managed to slam the door shut in his face without trapping one of us inside. Your worst nightmare. I gave the order to "kit up", shield, helmets the lot. It turned out he had spent all night sharpening a copper bracelet on the stone floor, the type you wear for rheumatism/arthritis into a handy blade that could inflict serious damage. Fifteen minutes later he was restrained, stripped, placed in a body belt and the six-inch shank recovered. Result.

Until the next time.

By now seg staff were having psychological assessments as to their suitability to work in the unit. God knows how some of us passed. Lots of macho-type lads thought they were capable of working the block, however, in reality very few cut the mustard. One such example was a loud scouser who boxed, even sparring with Nigel Benn back in the day.

Allegedly.

There was a tear-up on the yard. We split them up and the aggressor was held in locks on the floor. Without warning the prizefighter decided to dispense his own brand of justice to the pair. When we restrained him he was clearly shocked.

"Isn't that what happens down here?"

Needless to say he never worked in the seg again.

The Green Mile

We heard rumours coming out of HMP Wormwood Scrubs that prison officers had been suspended; they worked in the prison segregation unit. Talk was of an aggressive and brutal regime that existed in their block.

I rallied the troops into the adjudication room explaining that we ourselves would inevitably come under the spotlight. This had after all taken place in a seg unit that is often viewed by its very nature with a mixture of suspicion and envy by other staff. "I see us and them, the prisoners like the characters in *The Green Mile*." (Book 1996 Stephen King. Film 1999.)
This drew some muttering and strange looks, but I had their attention.
"We do our job that is often extremely challenging and difficult to the best of our ability. There is a fine line and we don't cross it. Otherwise, we have lost and are no better than them. So, let's just do it right and we will be fine."
Silence.
Blank faces, some nodding in agreement.
"Help me out here, lads. Tell me what you think."
Officer Lenny was the first to break the silence.
"You're right. But what I really want to know is, are you Tom Hanks?"

The senior officer at Wormwood Scrubs segregation unit was sentenced to four years imprisonment. Two fellow officers received four and three and a half years.

VIPs

The bright yellow Westland Wessex helicopter suddenly appearing out of the gloom hovered for a while before finally coming to rest on the grassed area alongside the car park outside the jail.

The entire prison dog section had been assembled for some time to act as guard of honour for the VIP guest. I was watching from my vantage point in the administration block, glad to be in the warm and away from the pomp and ceremony. The twenty or so handlers snapped to attention, looking very smart in their number one uniforms. The dogs were also immaculately turned out. All had been groomed specially for the royal occasion, a visit by HRH The Princess Royal, Princess Anne. They did however appear a little unsettled by the noise and air disturbance that the large helicopter was responsible for not fifty yards away. What had been a straight parade line was now resembling more of a crescent shape, with handlers desperately attempting to control their German shepherds. The princess stepped down from the machine holding on to her dress. An official-looking entourage gathered around her and they all proceeded to inspect the parade. Initially keeping at a safe distance, they had begun to relax when suddenly the fourth dog in line, barking uncontrollably, shot forward and leapt up at the startled VIPs, only to be pulled back in mid-flight by its clearly shocked and embarrassed handler who had stumbled and lost his peak cap in the process. This in turn set the other dogs off. The parade was turning into a shambolic affair, with Princess Anne being quickly led away to the safety of the jail.

Other visitors included the snooker trio of Jimmy White, Stephen Hendry and Marco Fu. They put on an exhibition match in the gymnasium for staff and prisoners. The ex-Manchester United and Aston Villa star turned TV presenter Dion Dublin was a frequent visitor. A really nice guy.

Walking out of the jail on a pleasant afternoon, alone, lost in my thoughts, I noticed a tall gentleman struggling to secure an

96

electronic gate. He was smartly dressed in a suit attempting to follow instructions being given to him via a gate intercom. This was unusual as most guests and visitors would be escorted. I guessed he was official and had been issued keys. The control room were talking to him be it through a muffled microphone. We were always on our guard for what was technically termed "a walkout" where a prisoner does exactly that, following a crowd or posing as an official or officer. Of course, there are layers of security procedures and measures in place. Biometrics, ID's, passwords etc. There is also human error but we were alert to this and today was no exception.

"Can I help you, sir?"

The man spun around, clearly frustrated at not having noticed me. He was middle aged, dark hair and beard and now much taller than I had at first thought.

"Thank you. I'm having trouble with this gate."

"Can I see some ID, sir?"

"Oh yes, of course". As he reached for his lanyard with ID attached, I began to think that he looked vaguely familiar. In fact, I was sure I recognised him.

"There you go, officer."

The photo ID matched the owner. I scanned it for his name. Terry Waite. The former Archbishop of Canterbury's envoy who had spent almost four years in solitary confinement in Beirut. As an envoy for the Church of England he had travelled to the Lebanon in an attempt to secure the release of four hostages, including the journalist John McCarthy. He himself was kidnapped and held captive until his release in 1991. I thought I knew him.

Here Come the Girls

Many operational female officers had now filtered into male prisons. Long Lartin was no exception. Initially they worked in the gate, reception and visits. As their numbers increased they inevitably found themselves on residential units, viewed at first with some scepticism by both staff and prisoners. They soon proved their worth. I personally felt they brought a calmer atmosphere and environment to the wings, chipping away some of the machoism that prevailed.

It was only a matter of time until a female officer was recruited to the unit. Officer Chantal was that officer, the very first to work in Long Lartin segregation unit.

Whilst being thrown about like a rag doll, the shirt being ripped off my back by a prisoner, Chantal pressed the alarm bell and leapt on the back of the con, all nine stone of her. She was indeed an asset to the team and was way better than any of us on the computer.

Exam time arrived at the end of June to be held at the Prison Officers Social Club. I felt it went well. I had worked hard and the results were published the following week. I had passed. Only four of the twenty were successful. After sitting a promotion board a month later, I was promoted to the rank of a substantive senior officer. Chantal had passed as well and was similarly promoted. She was moved to Delta Wing in her role as SO whilst I remained in the segregation unit for the time being.

Alpha Wing

After almost six years in the block I knew my time was up. Now it was onto a new challenge of a residential wing. I was to move to Delta as Chantal's opposite number meaning we worked opposite shifts and weekends. A date was set, my detail roster sorted, and I was ready to go. Then it all changed. The deputy governor came to speak with me the weekend before my move. He explained that I was going to work on Alpha Wing. The reason behind this was that SO Don had been badly assaulted and his opposite number had gone sick with stress.

"We need a strong SO to steady the ship. There are a lot of new inexperienced officers, Tom," said the deputy buttering me up, making me feel important.

"Alright, guv, no worries," I replied. I was confident.

During my time in the block I had experienced every kind of incident and scenario. How hard could it be? I soon discovered my new office was a mess where SO Don had been assaulted. A smashed computer, broken furniture, the telephone ripped out. No handover. The majority of staff were in probation and there was no leadership. I only knew a handful of staff and prisoners, the rest were distant and wary of the new senior officer that had arrived from the block. There was an atmosphere and tension. After a clearout of the offices, some fresh new equipment, even a large new roll board for the main office, I went in search of a "face" to measure the feelings of the prisoners on the wing. I soon found one.

Micky McAvoy, sentenced to twenty-five years for his part in the 1983 £26,000,000 Brinks-Mat gold bullion robbery at the Heathrow International Trading Estate. I didn't know McAvoy but I certainly knew who he was. We chatted and I found him to be a likeable character and easy to get along with. It became clear there was a distrust between prisoners and staff resulting in the assault of the SO, although he said that he didn't agree with it and was no party to it. Interestingly, he added that my appearance on the wing had increased the tension due to me coming directly to Alpha from the block as SO. I took his point explaining that I was both flexible and approachable. I knew that SO Don, as good a senior officer as he was, could be very rigid in his approach and dealings with cons and officers, possibly due to his strict military police background. I told McAvoy that I worked in a very different way.

"If liberties are taken by my staff or you lot, I will come down hard."

He understood my stance and agreed to spread the word.

Winning over the staff confidence was easy enough. They were keen and had a willingness to learn, allowing them some responsibility to make their own judgement. The prisoners were proving a tougher nut to crack. McAvoy was right, they distrusted me as much as I them. Quickly realising how institutionalised I had become myself by being in the block so long, I spoke with Micky McAvoy again, this time suggesting a football match strictly between Alpha Wing cons and officers. He was well up for it, even agreeing a side bet of a slab of Coca Cola from the prison canteen, enough for a can per player on the winning side. After much discussion it was decided that my team could have a couple of "ringers" to even things up. This idea proved to be the spark that lifted the general mood and atmosphere of the wing. Everyone was talking and looking forward to it. I roped in Officers Big Nige, Nobbie and Psycho Davies who was now known as "The General" by fellow officers, but still affectionately Psycho Davies by the cons. They were my three ringers as they were not employed on Alpha. A couple of solid centre backs and hopefully The General finding the back of the net as a striker.

It was a great game played on the association field with other wings watching and asking if they could play against their officers. We lost 2-1 but it wasn't about the result. Much more had been achieved than a football match. Prisoners were now openly engaging with staff on the wing. I paid my debt to Micky, placing the slab of Coca Cola, much to his amusement, in his bed whilst he was at work. He told me that he respected people who paid their debts on time. Even Ronnie O'Sullivan opened up to me.

Ronnie O'Sullivan Senior, father of six-time World Snooker Champion, Ronnie O'Sullivan Junior, had been sentenced to life in 1992 for the murder of Bruce Bryan, who was stabbed to death inside a club on Chelsea's Kings Road. Bryan was Charlie Kray's driver, the older brother of twins Ronnie and Reggie. Ronnie O'Sullivan Senior had been with me in the block for a while and we hadn't got along. It was a surprise when he began to talk with me on Alpha. Initially, he wanted to know what led to Officer Psycho Davies's hilarious collapse just ten minutes into the game. I told him that as per usual he had no ties for his football socks. He went into the gym and found a packing tape gun, the type you use to secure boxes. He wrapped the thick brown tape tightly around his sock, from the knee to the ankle. We all wore white socks, his were now brown plastic. When he finally ran out onto the pitch he looked ridiculous, casually shrugging off the usual abuse from his teammates and the cons. The game eventually kicked off when shortly after he lay on the pitch, screaming to referee PEI Martin that he couldn't feel his legs. The tightly wrapped plastic had cut the circulation. His socks and tape had to be cut free. Now unable to stand unaided he was quickly substituted, much to Officer Big Nige's relief who had questioned my selection to start with. O'Sullivan and I were laughing together as I relayed the full story. I took the opportunity to ask Ronnie why he felt free to speak openly to me now and not before.
"That was the block, boss. We were both living in a different world then."
After this conversation our relationship changed for the better. Ron was quick-witted and funny, often having the wing office in stitches of laughter.

He was released after serving eighteen years.

Nights

Night shifts in prison are not frequent affairs unless you work in the control room or are a dog handler, then they are one week in six on average. As senior officer on nights I was number two IC of the maximum security jail. A principal officer would be situated in the control room at night as everyone is locked up. It's a skeleton staff on duty, an officer on each wing, and one in each satellite area, such as the gate, hospital and segregation unit. The heart of the establishment at night is the emergency control room and the centre where I would be located with five officers. Outside in the grounds there were dog patrols. Long Lartin was one of only two jails in the country to be built with electronic locking, the other being HMP Gartree making them in effect doubly secure with manual locking running in tandem. Both jails were built of similar design, Gartree 1965, Long Lartin 1971. They look very similar. The electronic system was expensive to install and maintain, hence only two built. It allows for night sanitation.

At Long Lartin one prisoner from each landing on a residential wing can be released to use "night san". The prisoner simply presses a button in his cell allowing him to access the system. At busy periods, around 10pm for example, he would join a queueing system. When it is his turn the cell door clicks open allowing him access for up to twelve minutes at a time on that particular landing. After this time he would be told to return to his cell by the night officer on that wing. Prisoners would use the time allotted to visit the recess facilities even taking a shower, empty rubbish from their cell or simply talk to another prisoner through his cell door. This was seen by many as a safe option to exit the cell at night, safe in the knowledge you would be alone in the recess area. Of course, the system of "night san" is open to abuse, but generally it works. The control room has the power to restrict individual cells and landings or the entire wing from the facility. If a prisoner abuses this luxury, apart from the disciplinary proceedings being taken against him by the staff, he would face the wrath of his peers in their delay of night san. This system of access to night sanitation has allowed Long Lartin to continue with "slopping out" as there is no toilet or washing facilities in the cells, a procedure that has been condemned for years by successive inspectorates and governments.

There are occasions when it is necessary to enter a landing to deal with a prisoner who has for whatever reason not returned to his cell and closed his door. As the senior officer on nights this would mean calling a dog handler to the wing via the control room and entering the landing with centre staff. Prisoners may have smashed up the recess, self-harmed or lit fires etc. They are dealt with accordingly.

On one occasion I was called to A Wing where the prisoner had been out for half an hour. On arrival the officer informed us that he hadn't seen him at all. The control room couldn't raise a reply on the cell intercom system, yet his door was clearly open. I knew the con and had played short tennis with him in the gym. He was young but a big lad. I was fearing a heart attack. He certainly wasn't the self-harming or suicidal type. Quietly entering the landing, we checked the recess. No sign of him. Moving to his cell down the spur, I could see his door slightly ajar. Slowly pushing it open this giant of a man was lying motionless on top of his bed, fully clothed. I shook his foot to wake him. Suddenly he shot bolt upright, clearly in shock shouting out, which in turned made me jump back in fright knocking over an officer in the process. When we all calmed down and composed ourselves, he explained that he heard the door click open but must have fallen back to sleep. I told him that I thought our tennis days were over. He laughed replying, "You don't get rid of me that easy."

Night duty would be quiet or really busy, there never appeared to be a happy medium. Lucky for me, I often had quiet sets (seven nights on followed by seven rest days). We would raid the prison library to select videos and later DVDs, and Saturday night a takeaway, usually Indian, would be organised and delivered to the gate. Trivial Pursuit and Clag were all the rage in the early days. One officer who was training for the London Marathon would spend most of the early hours running around what was a 400m circuit of the corridors, whilst most of us would take the sensible option of sleeping.

The Wrong Taxi

Early one morning we had taken out a cat B prisoner who had claimed to have taken an overdose of prescription pills to hospital. There appeared to be genuine concern from our healthcare and the paramedics who were called into the jail. We eventually departed in an ambulance followed by the paramedics in their response car. This all turned out to be another waste of taxpayers' money. No overdose had in fact taken place as so often was the case. It always seemed as if no one was ever prepared to say no and call the prisoner's bluff. We were now left with getting a fit and able prisoner back to prison. The control room informed me Steve Selby (still Mayor of Evesham) would be along shortly to pick us up. He duly arrived apologising that he was not parked near the entrance to A&E explaining how busy it was outside. He was located in the main car park. I told Steve not to worry, we would go through the hospital to the main entrance and meet him there.

"Okay, I'll go and move the taxi to meet you as close as I can get," he said, and with that he was off.

We gathered our gear, I handcuffed the prisoner, then handcuffed him to another officer (double cuffed), said our goodbyes, thanked the staff and left. Once outside in the bright afternoon sunshine I was looking for Steve and his taxi. One of my colleagues spotted it and opened the back door for the prisoner to slide in, followed by the officer handcuffed to him. I opened the front passenger door. As I was getting in the driver was getting out. It wasn't Steve. We were in the wrong taxi. Worse still, it wasn't even a taxi, we were in a member of the public's car. I quickly got out attempting to explain myself to the driver who had now backed away from his own vehicle in shock. The two officers and prisoner were attempting to extradite themselves from the rear. Meanwhile, I caught sight of Steve waving and shouting at us frantically indicating his taxi. It was at this point I became aware that everyone around the congested hospital entrance was stood still in amazement watching the drama unfold. As we made our way over to Steve we were all laughing at our mistake, which just made matters worse as people stared even more. We quickly clambered into the correct taxi, still laughing and made a hasty exit.

Alpha Wing Part 2

Alpha Wing stabilised over the following months. SO Steve arrived and instantly proved to be very skilled in his abilities. We had been in the same class on our basic training course at Wakefield College back in early 1988. He had been posted to HMP Grendon, Buckinghamshire, initially. He slotted in a treat, easy going and very skilled in his dealing with people at all levels. That's all you need. There was an understanding and balance between us that allowed for a smooth running of the wing, something that was not always present on every wing.

Alpha at this time was proving so relaxed that Eddie Richardson even painted a mural of a man fly fishing on a river, a painting that remained on the wall for almost twenty years until an uncaring new breed of governing governor arrived and had it painted over, promoting everything as "new school" and crushing anything "old school" including the staff.

Eddie was a member of the infamous south London gang the Richardsons. Formed by his brother Charlie, the gang boasted such members as "Mad" Frankie Fraser and George Cornell, who nearly caused an all-out war between the Richardsons and the Krays' gang before his death when Ronnie Kray shot and killed him in 1966.

There was always an undercurrent of violence in prison despite outward appearances. These were seriously violent and dangerous individuals. Micky McAvoy wasn't called "Mental" Micky McAvoy for nothing. Whilst discussing the art of armed robbery with him he told me the secret to any robbery is to control the room and terrify the victims into doing what you want. For example, at Brinks-Mat the guards were tied up, blindfolded and then petrol was poured over them to reveal the combination of the vault.

"With the smell of petrol everywhere they couldn't give us the numbers quick enough," he said. "When one guard proved awkward I just started flicking an empty lighter by his ear. He soon told me what I wanted to know," joked McAvoy.

This lesson had been illustrated to me once before when a prisoner called Black Bob, due to his booming Black Country accent, had joined the queue for lunch at the hotplate. Bob was a prolific armed post office robber. Jokingly, a screw had said to him, "Go on, Bob, show us all how scary you are."
Bob appeared to go into role play for a moment, pulling up his donkey jacket collar, hunching up his shoulders, suddenly spinning around screaming at us behind the hotplate, "GIVE ME THE FUCKING MONEY!" whilst pretending to level a sawn-off shot gun at us. "GET ON THE FUCKING FLOOR!"
He was truly terrifying. Everyone froze for a few seconds while he was acting out his role, only he wasn't acting, this was his job.
"How was that?" he said proudly to the officer who had encouraged him in the first place.
"Fucking hell, Bob, I would have given you anything you wanted," the officer replied genuinely.
"Yeah, you would. Imagine if I had my stocking over my head and the sawn-off was real. Now give us double duff with me custard, guv."

The officer readily obliged the request to everyone's relief.

Foxtrot Wing. The Return

With two years completed on Alpha Wing, the powers that be were looking for a suitable senior officer to manage the basic regime on Foxtrot Wing. I knew a lot of the staff working Foxy. They tended to be more experienced officers. For me it was an easy decision to apply for the job. I got it, no problem. I didn't think there were too many other applicants to be fair. Running a strict regime was not to everyone's liking.

It was strange being back on the wing where it all began over twelve years earlier. Apart from the physical layout nothing was the same. The ground floor held vulnerable prisoners. These were cons who were in debt, sex offenders or, as was mainly the case, poor copers who would be extremely vulnerable to bullying if held on a normal residential unit. Upstairs were the basic regime prisoners that would arrive from other wings. An urgent referral would be made by a wing if an individual or group of prisoners were failing to conform to the regime of the establishment. For example, refusing to work, a positive mandatory drug test, a proven adjudication or a consistent general pattern of poor behaviour.

Any referrals were brought to the morning meeting and checked over by a rank no lower than a principal officer. If approved then the authorisation would be passed on to me in writing to organise the removal of the said prisoner to the basic regime on Foxtrot. Such a removal would normally take place as soon as the wing giving up its prisoner was secure. A C&R team would escort the con from his location to Foxy. The sight of a team in full kit and the shield would normally persuade the prisoner to co-operate and walk to his new location. Sometimes this was not the case and the prisoner would be restrained and removed in handcuffs.

When a new arrival came onto the unit he would be strip searched and handed prison clothing, only being permitted to wear his own trainers if he so wished. There would be no TV in the cell and he would only be allowed his most basic of possessions such as a radio, book, writing materials and such like. Exercise periods were limited as was association on the landing. To be fair, I was surprised how limited and austere the regime was. There was a great deal of discussion that the regime in the segregation unit was extremely similar. Proving my point, many prisoners would simply say "Take me to the block, guv, this is no better."

When prisoners progressed from the block to Foxtrot as part of their reintegration to general population, they would comment, "This ain't no halfway house, boss, should have stayed where I was."
It was more like a seg overflow but it worked. It was a deterrent. Prisoners who found themselves on the Basic Wing would have to conform for twenty-eight days before being considered suitable for a return to a residential wing. If they failed to adhere to the rules, another fourteen to twenty-eight days could be sanctioned.

I would lobby other senior officers to look at prisoners who were demonstrating a poor pattern of behaviour on their respective wings for referral, only too aware that I was working a wing with a capacity of seventy-plus. Our threes landing was empty. Unlike the daily dramas of a seg unit, this halfway house was easy to manage. Any real problem was simply moved on to the seg unit. My two years on the wing with experienced officers and a few, be it mildly uncooperative, cons were relatively easy going.

The number one governor at the time was a very capable and well-respected Jim Mullen. He was very firm but fair in his dealings with everyone. He was old school and I liked him and his approach. He told me he was under great pressure from the Home Office to "come into line when dealing with basic level prisoners." I asked him what this policy meant in the real world. He explained that he had fought to keep Foxtrot functioning as it was, but was inevitably fighting a losing battle.

"Tom, I retire in six months and then Foxtrot will revert back to a normal wing."

He continued, "Basic prisoners will be managed on their own wings as per policy. No carrot or stick anymore."

Relaying his thoughts to the staff brought about heated discussion as to the negative sides to such an argument. Levels of referrals to the basic regime would fall if they had to be referred and managed on their own wing. Where was the deterrent now? All these arguments would prove to be correct in time.

F Wing did indeed revert back and the number of basic prisoners being managed on wings throughout the jail plummeted. This all happened as Governor Mullen had predicted within a month of his retirement. The Home Office had scored a spectacular own goal. Years later the discussions would continue that the non-existence of a small basic unit was detrimental to the running of not just Long Lartin but any jail.

Bravo Wing

Two pleasant years had passed on Foxtrot but I needed more. The number one governor had warned me of the impending closure of Foxy in its present role. Despite excellent food served by an ex-chef who was now an officer and Sky football during our two-hour weekend lunch breaks, it was time to move on.

Bravo Wing had a good mix of experienced personnel and it needed it. The Home Office in its wisdom had ruled that all establishments would have an induction wing. Sounds great on paper. Yet another initiative dreamed up by civil servants who had little or no experience of actually working in a prison. The policy required all new receptions to complete an induction programme before they could be employed in a workshop or education. So far so good, in theory anyway. It also stated that all inductees be located on the same residential unit, being moved on when their two-week induction was completed. Long Lartin had allocated Bravo as its induction wing.

The reality of this process was flawed in its concept. All the issues and problems that a first night prisoner brought with him on arrival would be attempted to be resolved by the same wing and its staff, placing undue pressure upon us particularly when three or four new receptions turn up late in the day. They would often arrive with multiple problems and complex issues such as:

"Why the fuck have I been moved two hundred miles to a fucking supermax?"
"I haven't done anything, boss, why am I here in this gaff?"
"I need to phone my family and my legal team today, guv."
"Where is my fucking property? I want it now."
"I'm going to self-harm if you don't take me back."
"Where are my meds? I shouldn't be here."

If and when they actually completed their induction programme they would be required to relocate from Bravo to another wing. Of course, they eventually accepted their fate and became settled so moving them on proved difficult to the point of issuing direct orders. When such orders were refused it was stalemate. We couldn't move them all to the seg unit for refusing to relocate. It was an ongoing battle. The wing, as a result was always unstable due to its constant change in population. We were allowed a core group as permanent residents, wing orderlies and cleaners. This was the only stability we enjoyed, notwithstanding our protests to spread all new receptions around the jail. It fell on deaf ears. Senior management were adamant we would follow the process to the letter despite its obvious detriment to Bravo, staff, prisoners, and ultimately the establishment.

Gang Warfare

The population on Bravo eventually filtering to the rest of the jail was now changing. Gone were the armed robbers and IRA, being replaced by cocaine dealers and gang members belonging to groups such as "The Johnson Crew" and their rivals "The Burger Bar Boys." Now held at Lartin, these two black Birmingham based gangs were known for their drug dealing and gun crime. They came to the wider public's attention when a gunfight between the gangs left two innocent girls, seventeen year old Letisha Shakespeare and eighteen year old Charlene Ellis, dead on 2 January 2003. The gunfight took place for the retribution of the murder of a Burger Bar gang member a month earlier.

Crime that took place on our streets would be reflected in our jails a few years later. Now we had gang warfare openly existing inside and weapons were being manufactured at an alarming rate, makeshift shanks made from anything they could get their hands on. These were being carried "for protection, boss, like on the road. You get me?" we were constantly being told by cons. The workshop that repaired and refurbished push bikes had to close due to so many metal parts going missing and being turned into lethal weapons. This was despite upgraded searching procedures and aids such as wands and walk-through metal detectors similar to airports at massive financial cost. If it was metal it disappeared only to reappear as a blade or stabber. Finding metal harder to procure, hard plastic became the substitute (toilet brushes and toothbrushes).

Rivalries that had been removed from the streets over drugs, guns and postcodes were now reappearing in English jails up and down the country.

Prisoners on Bravo were gathering on the ground floor.
"Young men, gang affiliated, Tom," said Officer Kev nervously.
He was backed up by Officer Matt.

114

"They are milling about. Something isn't right."

I left my office to investigate. They were right. Around half of the wing was stood about on the ones. It was a standoff. There was a heightened tension that you couldn't fail to pick up on. Two of my female officers, Heather and Nicky, were surrounded by cons, all talking very loudly at once. Officers Paul and Rob were attempting to calm other prisoners in the foyer. The ones was equally crowded by cons.

This wasn't good.

I was aware of being watched. There were seven of us now with fifty cons invading our space. It was scary. An alarm bell sounded in the corridors and I'm thinking to myself, why the corridors?

Everything froze for a second then all hell broke loose. It was like the Wild West. Immediately, our alarm bell was pressed. Officer Nicky was on the floor, she had been pushed or fallen, I wasn't sure. She hadn't been assaulted; we weren't their focus. Officer Kev stood over her. We tried to split up the warring factions. Someone shouted at me, "Shall we draw batons?"

"NO!"

I felt it would make the situation far worse. The alarm bell sounded again. I made it to the stairs at the same time as prisoner Gary Nelson, street name Tyson, who was jailed in 2004 for life for possessing weapons and ammunition. In February 2006 Nelson was also found guilty of two counts of murder that he had carried out in October 1993 of a doorman at the Brixton Academy and a serving police officer. Stood side by side on the stairs, Nelson shouted at the cons to stop fighting, with me backing him up. It seemed to work. Glancing at each other, smiling, he said, "We've sorted it together, Tom."

Amazingly it was calming down and prisoners were wandering away. Comically, one prisoner who was just wearing a towel with shaving foam on his face and had been standing on the chest freezer watching the drama unfold, returned to the recess to continue his shower and shave. Other staff had finally started to arrive on the wing in a somewhat late response to the alarm bell being activated twice. It turned out they had already responded to an alarm in the corridors seconds before ours. Hence the delay. That situation had been a stabbing that had occurred while the mass movement of prisoners was taking place to the workshops. The corridors had to be cleared of prisoners. One con moved to the seg and one to the hospital. They had heard our alarm bell seconds later, wrongly assuming it was the same incident. Only when the control room informed officers with radios that there were actually two live alarm bell situations virtually in the same area at the same time did staff react and enter Bravo from the corridors.

As we reorganised ourselves the wing appeared to have returned to a relative calm. It seemed that whatever the prisoners were arguing about was settled for the time being. We started to relax. The brews were being handed around when Officer Kev handed me a shank. "A con just gave it to me."
On further investigation it turned out that it had been dropped or intentionally discarded during the melee.
"That could have been a lot worse," said Officer Matt sipping his tea.
We were all quietly thinking along the same lines. Someone broke the tension by asking Officer Kev why he had hold of the prisoner's legs who was stood on the freezer in just a towel and shaving foam whilst trying to protect Officer Nicky who was on the floor.
He laughed replying, "It's all about Health & Safety these days."
This lightened the mood and Bravo Wing returned to type.

The Inner Circle Crew

We were a tight crew on Bravo Wing, in particular my weekend division and we had to be as Bravo now had a street name, or rather two, "The Bronx" or "Beirut", whichever took your fancy. This wasn't a slur, everyone knew it was the toughest, least stable wing in the jail at the time. We just saw it as a badge of honour. I viewed it as a challenge and loved it. Residential discipline officers were split into two divisions as we worked an alternative weekend shift pattern. You have your division working with you exclusively Friday through to Tuesday. We worked, bonded and now socialised together including weekends off and trips to Blackpool to see the lights. Any excuse for a party. Our wing football team was the best in the jail and most of the prison team were selected from Bravo. If you were a decent player and officer then you would be actively recruited by me.

Officer Brian Psycho Davies's time was up on the DST. I wanted him as he had been an excellent seg officer and footballer despite his eccentric manners and behaviour. PO Geoff's views on the matter differed somewhat.
"You have got to be joking, we are not having that nutter on here."
I talked him round, explaining that once the staff were used to him and his ways he would be an asset to the wing and its football team. PO Geoff reluctantly agreed. "On your head be it, Hilly."
Brian proved to be a hit with the staff and cons, he was a good officer. His membership of Bravo's football team however wasn't always harmonious. I took great delight in reminding Geoff over a pint in the prison officers club about our discussion regarding him. "Yeah, but he's still a nutter, Tom."

Stood around the bar in Wetherspoons one evening talking football and inevitably about the wing, Officer Chris, who was a recent addition to Bravo and a valued new signing to the soccer team, piped up, "Have you guys heard? There is another gang on B Wing." We all stared at the newcomer in disbelief.

"What are they called?" enquired Officer Rob, who prided himself on his knowledge regarding gang affiliation, gang names, street names and codes.

Thinking for a moment Chris replied excitedly, "The Inner Circle Crew."

Roars of laughter followed helped on by the alcohol consumption. He looked embarrassed and confused. I put my arm around Chris's shoulder.

"That's us, we are the Inner Circle Crew," Officer Rob proudly informed him. He looked at me for reassurance.

"Yeah, he's right, it's what the cons call us."

He smiled. "I thought they were Yardies." More laughter.

"Am I part of the crew now?"

"Of course you are. Now get the beers in," said Officer Big Nige. Chris willingly obliged.

Officer Chris came from good stock. We met his dad SO Bob earlier in the book *Riot and Attempted Escape.*

Football's Coming Home

Kelly Dalglish is giving her morning 2006 World Cup report on Sky Sports News. At the conclusion she says to all England fans, "Get in your car/van whatever, get out here to Germany and join the party."

After studying the World Cup wall chart in Bravo's staff toilet and eventually finding an atlas in the prison library (try finding a map in a prison), plans were under way.

Officer Noel assured us he could borrow a minibus for the duration from his other boss at the coach firm he drove for part-time. Officers Paul, Rob, Dave, Matt x 2, Pete, Terry, mad Brian and the prison's Catholic priest Father Johnny would join us on our road trip. Big Nige was invited but declined saying, "I'm not driving halfway across Europe with mad Brian." Point taken.

We almost didn't make it across the Channel. Port authorities were convinced we were football hooligans, the minibus decked out with flags, inflatable spitfires, the stereo blasting out patriotic anthems and us playing football at the docks. I handed over eleven passports for rigorous inspection, informing the customs officers, "Kelly off Sky Sports told us to travel to the World Cup."
"Have you got tickets for any games?"
"No. We will go to the fan fests that the Germans are arranging and buy them off touts." There were stern, blank expressions. We were not going anywhere so there was only one thing for it.
"We are all prison officers, mate."
"Really? Show us some ID."
After which their attitude towards us changed and we were eventually allowed to board.

Mad Brian immediately began to entertain the ship's passengers by organising a quiz that he had prepared, handing out pens and paper from Bravo wing's stationery cupboard to bemused guests aboard the ship. As always, after the initial shock the public warmed to him.

Officer Paul said, "He'll be singing to them in a bit."

Sure enough, after the completion of the quiz he swapped his Brazil top for a Wales shirt and bellowed out Tom Jones' "*Green, green grass of home*" to rapturous applause.

Arriving in Nuremberg, southern Germany, the campsite is packed. Directed to a kids play area complete with sandpit, swings and climbing net we pitched our tents. Paul and I take ourselves off to explore and locate the shower block. Everywhere is shaven heads and tattoos.

"They all look like ex-cons."

I have to agree. The shower block is flooded and two ex-cons are using a standpipe with a hose attached as a makeshift shower. They spot us and the one taking a shower jokes, "This is worse than prison showers."

We laugh uneasily and agree with them. Paul was right.

Making our way back to camp at the sandpit we are stopped dead in our tracks. Mad Brian is at the top of the climbing net having attached a huge banner clearly made of prison bedsheets. He is attempting to unfurl it assisted by our new Dutch neighbours. Everyone is stood back waiting to see what it says. As he sees us he shouts, "What do you think? I got the lads to make it for me in the laundry."

With that he lets it drop. It reads, **HMP LONG LARTIN ON TOUR.**

We both shout back in unison, "Get that fucking down!"

We would continue our excursions around Europe together over the next ten years visiting Germany, Austria, Switzerland, Poland, Ukraine and France.

Muslim Extremists and Radicalisation Part 1

As well as gang members from Britain and around the world, we had another gang that was growing at an alarming rate. Muslim extremists. It was becoming an ever-increasing issue for the prison service who continually struggled to deal with this sensitive situation.

In the 1980s Muslim prayer would consist of a few prisoners being accommodated in a side office off the education block on a Friday afternoon. Now, both the Roman Catholic and Church of England chapels were filled for prayer on Fridays. The Christian artifacts were covered with sheets and the floor space filled with prayer mats. Long Lartin now employed two full-time imams and one part-time. No one objects to any person freely practising their chosen religion including those who find themselves incarcerated. The problem that was becoming clearly evident within prisons the length and breadth of the country was that prisoners were being radicalised by Muslim extremists. They were being threatened, bullied, coerced, conned, tricked and forced into following and actively participating in another faith that they had clearly not chosen for themselves. Many victims of this radicalisation were vulnerable and some very dangerous. Appearing at Muslim services were British males who had never visited any church in any capacity before. They were dressed in traditional Islamic clothing, their heads shaved and many had grown long beards. Weeks before they were wearing Nike tracksuits or their favourite football shirt. Shockingly, many had adopted traditional Muslim names. Chris Jones had become Ahmed Mohammed. Even more shocking, the prison service allowed this to flourish, supported, even encouraged by the government of the day, saying, "We don't have a problem in our jails with radicalisation."

Meanwhile, the war rages on in Afghanistan.

Old School

There were still one or two old school cons at Long Lartin, men who over time had come to earn my respect and me theirs. This may sound strange, even unsettling to some, but it is human nature. If someone treats you how you wish to be treated then it becomes reciprocal. I make no apologies for this point of view, we just called it respect.

Charlie Kray was one of these men. I got to know him in Lartin. He had been sentenced in 1997 to twelve years for his role in plotting to bring £39,000,000 of cocaine into the country claiming he was set up by the police. He was sentenced at Woolwich Crown Court aged seventy and died three years later. A polite, respectful and likeable man. Reggie Kray was also held at Long Lartin during the early 1980s before my time, often on "lie downs" from other dispersals.

Billy Tobin – all of the above and more. A true gentleman and a character, not to mention a prolific armed robber in his heyday. Over a five-year period spanning the late 1970s and early 1980s, William Tobin had been charged five times with five major crimes and five times had been acquitted by juries. *The Sun* newspaper dubbed him "Billy Liar", we called him Billy, our number one orderly on Bravo Wing. I called him Bill. Bill will appear later in this book. In the meantime characters such as Micky McAvoy and Billy Tobin are discussed at length by former criminal and Micky's nephew, John McAvoy whom I never met inside, in his excellent and inspiring book *Redemption. From Iron Bars to Ironman.* Bill's personality leapt off the pages when I read it. It was if he was talking directly to me.

"To thrive in our world you have to get on with anyone. You can be in a boozer with a bunch of thugs one day or the Pont de la Tour, Tower Bridge, with barristers and brokers the next. The most important thing of all is loyalty, respect. Your name, your reputation is everything. If your name is shit then so are you and you never hurt women or children. If you have an

122

issue with someone, you deal with them. You never touch their family. People think its old-fashioned but this is our code and it's set in fucking stone".

Pulp Fiction

A long bank holiday weekend at the conclusion of the football season. The divisional play-off finals were in full swing culminating with the Championship final for Premier League status. In prison bank holidays can drag on. Unlock, full association, no work or routine doesn't suit everyone, particularly if you are not interested or do not participate in exercise or sport. Boredom sets in. This often results in trouble.

Watching the League Two play-off final in the association room on Bravo with Officers Paul, Rob and Big Nige along with a dozen prisoners, it's a calm, relaxing afternoon despite both the officers and cons continually pointing out how poor the level of football is in the lower leagues. This is all for my benefit as a Bristol Rovers fan. Rovers always compete in the lower pyramid of the football league, as opposed to them all supporting Premier League clubs even if they are WBA and Aston Villa.

Officer Paula walks in bringing half time brews accompanied with cakes and biscuits.
"It's all quiet downstairs, most are out in the sunshine on the wing exercise yard."
"Thanks, Paula, it's all quiet up here too."
She laughs adding, "Will you four be up here all weekend watching the play-offs?"
Officer Paul replies, "Not if it's as fucking bad as this game."
Another swipe at lower league football. They just don't get it.

The cons are drifting back in for what we all hope will be second half excitement, having been told by Officer Paula in no uncertain words to go and make their own half time brews. One of them, who had a scary close resemblance to Samuel L. Jackson's character Jules Winnfield in the 1994 film *Pulp Fiction*, moves toward the huge television positioned on the equally large table and says, "Boss, there is something under the TV." He then starts to investigate despite all our protests as the game has just resumed.

Officer Paula says, "Tom, he's right. There is something." The Jules Winnfield lookalike turns to us brandishing a huge shank, holding it above his head and begins to recite lines from his character in the film.

"I will strike down upon thee with great vengeance and furious anger, those who would attempt to poison and destroy my brothers."

Following an uneasy silence at the conclusion of his speech, he bursts out laughing and hands me the shank, to everyone's relief. I congratulate him on his find, offer him some cake and place the weapon safely under my seat. We all then continued watching the football, which doesn't get any better.

Lazy Sunday Afternoon

Sunday afternoon, Bravo Wing, the alarm bell rings out. I rush upstairs with Officers Kev, Matt and Mike. We see a young black prisoner being helped by Officer Paula and other cons. He has been slashed across his face. There is so much blood that his sky-blue prison issue T-shirt is now red. I instruct Matt to stay with Paula and get the victim immediately off the wing to healthcare. Meanwhile, Officers Kev and Mike have gone looking for the perpetrator. I notice a trail of blood on the stairs leading to the threes landing and I investigate the splashes of blood that lead to the threes recess. Heart pounding, I enter cautiously. Someone is in the shower area.

It's Warren Slaney, convicted of the so-called "Hot Dog" murders in 1990. In 1992 he was given a double life sentence for the murders of Gary Thompson and his business partner John Weston. Thompson owned a fleet of fast-food vans. The killers stole takings of up to £60,000 and left both men dying of shotgun wounds. He doesn't communicate with screws unless he has to. Normally he is a four man unlock located in the segregation unit. This is a brief spell for him on normal location. It's about to end.

Slaney is frantically shoving his bloodstained clothing out of the small, barred shower room window in a vain attempt to destroy evidence. We are alone. He has his back to me not realising my presence. Heart still pumping, my adrenalin high, I simply say, "Warren, calm down." He immediately spins around to face me. He is covered in the victim's blood and he still has the blade in his hand. I tell him again to calm down, he too is clearly pumped with adrenalin.

"Sit down on the bench, Warren, and put the knife on the floor," I quietly tell him. To my surprise he does. I slowly approach Slaney and kick the weapon clear. Staff are on the landing now; we both hear them enter the recess. I tell him we will walk to the block together. He just stares at me the entire time saying nothing. I let the staff know our whereabouts. He is told to stand, face the wall and handcuffed. I keep my promise and walk with him to the block.

On my return to the wing Billy Tobin is busy mopping up blood trails.
"Bad business that, Tom, best get yourself a cup of tea."
"Yeah, I think I will, Bill."

Rat Scabies

Whilst writing up a report that would most certainly end up in some cloud or other, an officer breezed into my office with a welcome coffee. As he placed the cup down he noticed the small circular rash on the inside of my wrist. I told him it was nothing and that it had only appeared the previous day. The following morning an identical sized rash had appeared on the inside of my thigh. Time to revisit the doctor's surgery.

Examination complete, the doctor made a call to a colleague, checked the internet then reached for a dusty medical book. After flicking through a couple of pages he had clearly confirmed the prognosis. "Scabies," he proudly announced. What?! I had heard of Rat Scabies, drummer for the late seventies punk band The Damned, which didn't bode well. He continued to explain excitedly, probably due to this being a rare and ancient affliction, that he clearly didn't come across it every day.
"Submariners are prone to catching it on submarines due to their living in close proximity. It is also prevalent in institutions like…" He hesitated whilst searching for a good example. I helped him out.
"Like a prison?"
"Exactly that," he replied, adding the question, "Where do you work?" despite him already knowing the answer I suspected.
"It's highly contagious, though simple to treat with a course of medication."

Signed off for a week on sick leave I contacted the jail. After the initial piss taking they told me that there had indeed been a "limited" outbreak with some prisoners being isolated in the prison hospital, adding that the plan was to keep it quiet so as not to create panic. I wasn't sure if this was the correct strategy. Hell, what did I know?

I felt fine despite the ugly rash spreading across my chest. The doc had said it would get worse before it got better and then disappear by the week's end. He was right. It started to clear up as the course of medication took hold. In fact, he was spot on. It was extremely contagious spreading throughout the prison like an epidemic.

Much later the service will struggle as the world does to contain and manage another pandemic.

Officer X and Prisoner Y. Part 1

Officer X arrived on Bravo directly after her initial training. She was in her late thirties originating from Bristol. We got along straightaway. In fact, she instantly gelled with her peers both male and female and was a positive addition to the wing. Her enthusiasm and willingness to learn was infectious and she was confident in her dealings with prisoners right away. She was strict, fair and showed compassion where appropriate. We all respected her for this approach. A popular and trusted member of the team, she threw herself wholeheartedly into the job.

X made no secret that her personal life was tough, often requesting roll checks, early starts and late finishes to work in addition of her thirty-nine hours as overtime. In my capacity as wing detail manager, this was easy to facilitate. The early starts and late finishes were unpopular with the majority of staff, so she picked up the slack. Questioning her motives she would reply, "I'd rather be here than home, and besides I enjoy it and need the extra money." This work ethic further improved her relationship with staff. On social nights out as part of the Inner Circle Crew, she would fit right in and party with the rest of us.

Her probationary period almost complete, she approached me suggesting that she take over B Wing's "tea-boat".
"It's in a right state, there is no coffee, money is owed, and we didn't have a cooked breakfast last weekend."
I jumped at her offer. She was the person to turn it around. I knew full well she would get the money owed from the staff. Officer Chris was frankly hopeless at collecting the subs from the likes of Officers Big Nige and Brian. Within a week the tea-boat fortunes had been completely reversed. Milk, tea, coffee, soft drinks, cereal, new pots and pans, the lot, and there was a full English breakfast both supplied and cooked by Officer X at weekends. Result! I told her to make sure she had collected all monies owed explaining that I didn't want her subsidising the cost.

"Don't worry, they have all coughed up, Tom, even Big Nige. We're in profit now."

Next she requested that she overhaul the cleaning store.
"We have a security audit coming up, it really needs sorting."
She was right and I knew it, but I was hesitant that she was taking on too much responsibility. There was a second reason. I didn't like the idea of female officers alone in the cleaning store with prisoners. However, our number one cleaner at that time was a trusted cat A. Prisoner Y. I spoke to them both and we agreed to her new role as Bravo cleaning officer. She was thrilled, promising to repay my faith and trust in her by ensuring we pass the audit.

Within weeks the cleaning store was updated, everything in order, shadow boards painted, tally systems, tool inventories, ordering systems, all fully functional. The wing cleaners and painters had transformed the wing, all under the watchful eyes of Officer X and prisoner Y who had formed the seemingly perfect partnership. We breezed the security audit achieving a ninety-five per cent score, much to the delight of the governing governor who personally praised myself, Officer X and even prisoner Y.

Then the bubble burst.

Prisoner Y was caught in possession of a phone charger and immediately moved to segregation pending adjudication.

Officer X unexplainedly became unsure of herself, questioning if she had in fact passed her probation. I reassured her that she had. She continued on this thread, asking if our security department had any reservations about her. I again found myself reassuring her saying, "I'm sure they hadn't any concerns."

Meanwhile, prisoner Y, who was meant to be shipped out of Long Lartin, was now only going to be moved to another wing.

Officers Big Nige and Paul speak with him in the seg unit and relay to me that if we allow him back on Bravo he will repay us with information to our and the establishment's benefit. Weary of this option I discuss it with the number one governor, who ultimately leaves the decision with me saying "perhaps better the devil you know." After a discussion on the wing we decide to accept prisoner Y back to the fold, much to Officer X's delight. I go myself to the seg to pick him up. He is overjoyed to see me. He has a quick chat with the seg governor who emphasises to him how lucky he is to be returning to Bravo and having a second chance. We walk back together.

Within half an hour of returning prisoner Y knocks on my office door. Still dressed in his seg clothes he pulls a formidable blade from his tracksuit, proudly laying it on my desk saying, "I will have the wing clear of weapons and drugs within the week," enthusiastically shaking my hand and thanking me for giving him the opportunity to redeem himself. I explained that I was off on leave for two weeks summer holiday, instructing him who to approach with his finds. I thanked him for his co-operation.
"I promised, it's the least I can do. Have a good leave, guv."
At lock up I briefed the staff as to what had happened and what had been agreed between us leaving the jail on a high for two weeks in the sun, having no idea that on my return it would all have imploded spectacularly, leaving me with some explaining to do.

Officer X and Prisoner Y. Part 2

Returning home from holiday my answerphone was full of messages, the red light flashing non-stop in the hallway. I immediately called Big Nige, he would know what was going on. After enquiring how the holiday was which I thought odd in itself as he would see me on Monday, he got to the point.

"Our so-called friend X has been bringing stuff in."

I was speechless and a wave of emotions washed over me. What? When? Where? How? All the questions were fired at him at once. Anger had taken over. He said that he was as surprised and shocked as I was, all the staff on Bravo were, no one on the wing had suspected her of any wrongdoing.

"What the hell happened then, Nige?"

He told me that security had been tipped off by a prisoner that she was smuggling in mobile phones worth £500 a time, SIM cards, chargers and alcohol. The DST with a drugs dog had caught her at the gate on her commencement of a shift at midday. She was attempting to bring in vodka mixed with orange in large orange squash five litre containers. Security escorted her to her car where they discovered SIM cards and brand-new mobile phones. Apparently, she became obstructive quoting her so-called "rights" when the drugs dog searched the car. I was speechless. Nige continued. "There is more." She was in league with prisoner Y, they were in partnership. She had smuggled the goods in and he sold and distributed them. Bravo Wing was locked down and had been for three days now. Mobile phones had been thrown from cell windows as a full standdown search was taking place, conducted entirely by the DST and security. Nige said, "No discipline officers are involved with the searching, Tom. They don't trust us."

"I'm sure they don't. Can you blame them? It's understandable under the circumstances."

I could tell from his tone he was as shocked and angry as myself. My closing line to Nigel was, "Nige, if you were a bent screw you know I would shop you, don't you?"

"He replied, "Yeah, and if it were you I'd grass you up too."

I knew he wasn't lying.

"See you Monday, mate," I said hanging up.

The weekend passed in a blur. I felt so let down after the anger subsided. I had placed my trust and friendship with her as had others on Bravo. I knew they felt the same.

Monday morning arrived. I drew my keys reporting directly to the wing. The gossip was rife all over the jail. B Wing was unlocked now but the mood was subdued. Prisoner Y's cell had been searched and had been sealed by security. He had been ghosted out of Long Lartin immediately. As I suspected, the staff felt, as I did, cheated and angry. Suspicion fell on us all. Prisoners were talking now telling us that they had been threatened by prisoner Y and Officer X and were unwilling to say anything at the time due to their influence. It was all extremely hard to accept. What else had been smuggled into the establishment? Drugs or worse? I didn't want to contemplate the reality.

Mid-morning I was summoned to the number one governor's office. I had been expecting it. What I wasn't expecting was the presence of the security governor. I was in for a grilling.
The number one governor opened up with, "What I see is a triangle with Officer X and prisoner Y at the base and you, Tom, at the apex."
Stunned at first, I said nothing. Then it was the security governor's turn.
"Why was she a cleaning officer? Why was she in charge of your staff tea-boat? Why so many early starts and late stay backs?"
Now it was my turn, explaining myself fully to the pair. I stood up, faced the number one gov and said, "Hindsight is a wonderful thing. You know I'm not a bent screw, none of us on Bravo saw this, not even officers Heather, Miriam, Nigel or Paul. All experienced and trusted colleagues."
The number one replied, "You're right, I know that cause if I didn't you wouldn't be here. So fuck off back to your wing and run it like I know you can."

Returning to the wing the fallout continued. Prisoners were freely talking to us now explaining the grip the pair had over them. Nine mobile phones had been found discarded outside Bravo in the grounds. The security principal officer gave us more of an insight during a hastily arranged meeting with the staff. Alcohol had been found in the cleaning store hidden with cleaning fluids stored in secure lockers that X had the keys to. Incriminating notes between X and Y were found in his cell. We were then informed by the PO that at weekends, when X brought all of our tea-boat supplies into the jail with many of us meeting her at the gate lodge to assist, we were actually carrying in mobiles concealed inside industrial sized coffee tins. No wonder I was questioned about her position as a cleaning officer and her role running our tea-boat. Staff looked at each other in disbelief as he continued. Then another bombshell. "We are still awaiting her formal resignation," he said.

No charges were ever brought against her, the service brushing it all under the carpet to save the embarrassment and publicity.

How times change. Within months of X walking away the charge of "misconduct in a public office" was in vogue. Public officials, such as police and prison officers were being found guilty and receiving jail time.

Grant Mitchell

X finally resigned and out of the blue I got a text.
Meet me, I will tell you everything. I'm sorry. It was sent from X.
My mind was spinning and I didn't sleep well that night. Should I approach security and seek permission? They wouldn't allow it. If I agreed to meet her perhaps she would tell me the truth. Did she bring drugs? A firearm? Or ammunition in? I had to know or at least try and find out. Reluctantly, I texted back arranging to meet at a local pub garden. I told no one.

Cycling to the pub on a day off around midday, I was extremely anxious. Arriving early, I sat in the garden by the river with my pint. It was a pleasant day, bright and sunny. If I wasn't so nervous it would have been enjoyable. Two workmen were repairing a thatched roof on a cottage next to the pub, otherwise I was alone.

My mobile rang. It was a number I didn't recognise. I answered. A young girl's voice asked, "Tom? Are you at the pub?" It wasn't Officer X.
"Yes. Who is this?"
The mystery voice said, "We will be there shortly," and hung up. Panicked by this call, I was about to leave when a car raced into the car park. It was Officer X's vehicle but she wasn't driving. A male driver who looked like Grant Mitchell from the TV soap drama *EastEnders* and just as angry was accompanied by a girl that I recognised as Officer X's daughter. I had met her at a Bravo football match the pair had watched at the social club a couple of weeks earlier. She was aged around fifteen and was now pointing me out to Grant Mitchell. I stood up as the car screeched to a halt. The driver's door flew open and Grant leapt out. The young girl followed.
Grant shouted, "YOU GRASSED HER UP!"
Before I could reply he ran at me, punching me to the floor. The daughter screamed and shouted for her dad to stop. I

picked myself up. Attempting to calm him down and knowing my jaw was broken with blood pouring out of my mouth, the workmen shouted from the rooftop of the thatched cottage and the barman came out of the pub. I indicated to them it was over and not to call the police. Grant gave the young barman a single glance and he swiftly returned inside. The roofers continued with their work. Just about able to talk I motioned the pair to sit down, telling Grant that if he went for me again I would dive into the river to escape him. Sat around the beer table he told me that he was Officer X's husband. I had guessed that for myself. I was in pain and just wanted to get to hospital. I asked him straight out what she had brought in. He told me what I already knew so I pressed him further.

"What about drugs?"

"No," he said.

I didn't trust him.

"It started off with just some alcohol, then he got her," meaning prisoner Y. "She was too frightened to speak to you cause you would have turned her in."

Too right, I thought, though I said nothing. I didn't believe anything he was telling me. Feeling sick and nauseous I stood up.

"We're done here, I'm going to get my teeth fixed."

As I walked away pushing my mountain bike across the car park, the workmen watching from the roof, I was thinking how I was going to explain all of this.

Attempting to cycle the six miles back home, I was in no fit state to ride but I didn't fancy the walk either. I pedalled on. Whilst wobbling up the slightest incline an anonymous white van sped past, his close proximity and resulting slipstream causing me to clip the kerb. Somehow, I stayed upright and made it to my village.

This close encounter with the van would be my alibi.

I spotted a friendly neighbour who quickly grasped my situation and took me to Worcester Hospital. They confirmed my fears.

A broken jaw. I was given painkillers, cleaned up and admitted to a ward. An operation to plate and repair the jaw would be performed the following morning. Whilst I was trying to rest in the evening, my phone flashed.

If you report me to the police for assault we will report you to the prison, the message read, sent from X's phone. Report me for what? Fuming I replied, *Enough, it's finished. I haven't and won't call the police. Leave me alone.*

Discharged the following evening, feeling very sore and bruised with a plated and wired jaw, my wife drove me home. I couldn't and didn't say much. She, on the other hand, was positively chatty.

"The prison has arranged for the police to interview you and take a statement about that van knocking you off."

I couldn't believe my ears. "WHAT?!"

"It's very nice of them to sort it out, don't you think? I'll bake a cake, they're coming tomorrow about 4pm."

The cake baked, proudly displayed, tea made in a teapot, they arrived as promised at 4pm. I was very cagey. Saying that I had nothing really to say was a pointless exercise. The police on the other hand were intent on writing a statement so I reluctantly went along with it. What choice did I have? My wife was pouring tea for the two policemen while my daughter was showing them her doll's house. It of course turned out to be an extremely vague statement about a mysterious white van, registration and driver unknown. I thanked them for their time and got rid of them pronto.

Officer X and Grant Mitchell. Part 3

The wing trundled on through summer and I felt we had finally achieved a status quo, putting the Officer X and prisoner Y events firmly behind us. The Bronx had faded into Bravo once more, fresh receptions and incidents but generally the ship was steady.   PO Geoff was off on long-term sick and I felt I was ready to step up. There had been a promotion board held for the rank of principal officer before Geoff left and I felt it had gone well. It was a case of wait and see. I certainly had "plenty of operational experience" the board had relayed to me. There was no doubting that.

A new wing governor turned up on Bravo. At first I thought he would be a help, bridging the gap to the senior management team as we had no PO. How wrong could I be? He had been promoted via the dog section at some sleepy hollow. Nothing against dog handlers you understand, but this one had made it into a suit and was clearly way out of his depth. He gathered us together in the wing office and introduced himself.
"I will visit the wing each day to address any problems you may have."
Staff looked at one another in that knowing way. Officers Paul and Matt were doing their upmost not to laugh. Big Nige got in first.
"With respect, sir, we have heard it all before. If you make it here every day till Friday it will be a miracle."
Paul was sniggering now, so were one or two others.
"Okay, Nige, let's just give the gov a chance," I said.
In typical Nigel fashion he said, "Fair enough, Tom, I'll give him till Friday."
This introduction was descending into a farce when Officer Phil enquired what residential experience the new gov had. Where had he been prior to Lartin? Twenty years on the dogs and some jail we had never heard of wasn't going to cut it. Making his excuses he quickly left the wing leaving Officer Phil without answers.
Big Nige said, "That's it. We'll never see him again."

He was right. We didn't.

The phone rang. It was the governor's secretary. "The number one governor would like to discuss something with you, Tom, in his office at 10.30," she said. That was it. I called Officers Paul, Rob and Nigel into my office telling them that the governor was going to offer me promotion to principal officer.
Paul said, "That's great, maybe you can stay on Bravo till Geoff comes back."
"That makes sense. I'm sure that is what'll happen."
Paul shook my hand congratulating me. The others followed suit.

Arriving at the number one's office, the governor's secretary ushered me in. Something wasn't right. The gov was looking at me sternly and why on earth was the security governor there? I would soon find out. I hadn't even been offered a seat. He had a handwritten letter in front of him.
"Officer X has written to me," he began.
I couldn't believe what I was hearing.
He continued, "Tell me the truth, Tom, don't lie to me."
I told him that I had no intention or reason to lie. I was puzzled. He explained she had told him in the letter that my broken jaw had come about from her husband assaulting me and not as I had made out. I was confused. Why on earth would she say this six months on? What did she hope to gain? I felt sweat in the small of my back, the gov's eyes boring into me awaiting my response. I broke the silence.
"Yes, that's true. That's what happened."
I felt relieved.
He was angry.
The security governor spoke. "So you lied to the police, Tom?"
"What choice did I have? I didn't want to speak to them, you called them in."
They didn't appreciate my tone. I couldn't see a problem. They were making one.
"PERJURY!" shouted the number one. "I have called in the police. They will give you a formal caution. Now get out."

140

I left his office feeling angry and let down. Why on earth aren't the police talking to X and Grant Mitchell. I was the victim.

I didn't give a toss about what the gov or police thought, what mattered was what Paul and Nigel would think. I soon found out.

Anticipating good news and a promotion party, staff were shocked to see my demeanour on my return. They brought me back to reality and made everything seem better by laughing at my misfortune, latest predicament and generally taking the piss. Situation normal.

A day or two passed when Officer Paul burst into the office and excitedly announced that "the Old Bill are at the gate to interview you."
Fuck it, I was secretly hoping the number one gov had been bluffing.
"Go and get them, I'll be..." he was on his way before I finished my sentence.

The police could not have been more understanding.
"Embarrassed to even being called to speak to you," one of them told me.
"It's your bloody number one governor pushing it," said his colleague.
I explained that governing governors, particularly at a category A establishment, were a law unto themselves. Liken them to King John without the Magna Carta. This brought a smile to the cops.
"Yep, our governor couldn't believe what your gov wants either. So, here's what we propose."
They then explained that a formal caution was out of the question.
"We will simply issue you a fixed penalty notice, similar to a parking ticket."
One of them pulled out a book of tickets that looked exactly like parking fines.

"We issue them to youths who graffiti or vandalise bus shelters."

"What, like an ASBO?" I asked, not really sure.

"No, like a parking fine," they said.

"Brilliant, can I pay now?"

"No. You have to pay it through the council. It's £80," they said handing me my ticket.

"Okay. Thanks, lads, I really appreciate this."

"No problem. Hopefully it will satisfy your governor."

"Yeah, don't worry, I'll be staying out of his way."

Officer Paul was attempting to open the office door with a tray of brews and biscuits. I beckoned him in, Nigel was right behind him.

"Good news. Nigel, you have to write a cheque for £80 and get this off to the censors for posting. It's my ASBO. I'll give you £80 cash. I can't have an odd council payment showing up on my bank statement. My missus will spot it. She works in finance," I told the coppers.

They laughed whilst one of them dropped his biscuit into his tea. We all laughed.

I kept the receipt of my fixed penalty issued to me by the police in my uniform ready to produce at a moment's notice to the number one if and when I saw him. Bearing in mind I was actively avoiding him, I couldn't wait to tell him how the police had dealt with me. It didn't take long. Entering the jail early one morning I spotted him going upstairs from the gate to his office. I caught up with him on the stairs.

"Gov, the police just gave me a fixed penalty," I told him smugly adding, "like a parking fine."

He turned and scowled at me as I handed him my copy. He studied it, shook his head in disbelief and forcing it back into my possession continued to his office, obviously disgruntled. Number one governors are used to having it all their own way.

Perrie Wing

Football had taken its toll on my right knee. It required an operation to the ACL (anterior cruciate ligament) then a long period of rest and recuperation. Three to four months off work. Having served close to six years on Bravo it was decided that on my return I would be moved to the operations group. Working within this group wasn't ideal, I had only ever worked residential units. I was a prison officer. My present goal was to have the op, recover and get fit again.

All went well, recovery was on track and it was almost time to get back. Officer Paul phoned excitedly telling me there was a position for me on a wing. Himself, Officer Matt (both of them), Kev and Mike were on the move from Bravo to Perrie Wing. There was a vacancy for a senior officer. Furthermore, he had had words with the PO. If I rang him confirming my interest the position was mine.
"We can all go there together, working the same weekend. What do you think?"
"Yeah. Cheers, Paul. I'll call PO Mark right away. That's great news, thanks."
I did however have some reservations. As much as I was desperate to remain on res units, Perrie Wing would be a very different experience. Calling up PO Mark straight after my conversation with Paul proved advantageous.
"When can you start?"
"Monday morning suit you?"
"Nice one, Tom. See you then."

Perrie Wing was named in honour of Bill Perrie who retired from the prison service in 1978. He was a former Long Lartin governing governor. The wing was opened in 1999 alongside a supermax segregation unit (the largest in Europe). They both substantially increased the capacity of Long Lartin. I had seen the wing under construction some eight years earlier. The outside wall had been opened up at the back of the jail, and another gate lodge had been constructed strictly for the use of contractors in their construction of the new wing and segregation unit. Once the foundations were laid the building quickly took shape. The cells arrived preconstructed, similar to Lego bricks on huge flatbed, articulated lorries. They were winched into position by an equally giant crane. The new wing and seg unit were connected to the existing jail by means of a secure concrete and steel walkway, similar to the new gymnasium. Land had always been a premium at Lartin, with acres of open space to develop within the walls. It was always just down to funding.

In 1999 there had been an open evening for families to show off the new wing. I took this opportunity to invite my dad to the jail. He made similar comments to that of my brother, who I had taken around some years earlier.
"It looks like your old school, son."

Monday morning arrived with me checking out my new place of work.

Perrie Wing was split into two units – Perrie Red Spur: ninety prisoners. Perrie Blue Spur: forty-five prisoners. They may have been referred to as spurs but for all intents and purposes they were two separate units managed by a single senior officer. This was an ongoing problem for the two years I spent there. I was continually moving between the two, usually looking for staff. Blue Spur was now to be the new induction unit, the real reason that myself and a few ex-Bravo staff found ourselves here. It was a small, manageable unit. Unlike Red Spur, both were spread over two landings. All cells had in-cell sanitation and were considerably larger than those on the old wings. There were no expensive electrical locking systems, just old-fashioned manual locks. I was very aware now of human error. There were no failsafe's here unlike the old wings. Senior management were beginning to treat and view staff much like robots, not humans, who can make mistakes.

The relatively new and quiet Blue Spur induction wing almost ran itself due to its size. Similar to Bravo, we had issues moving prisoners on once they had completed induction. Now they didn't want to relocate to an old wing and slop out.

Red Spur was busy and very noisy due to its size and open landings. It wasn't popular with staff either as the majority wanted to work the smaller unit.

Daily detailing proved to be a headache. I would often rotate staff between the two spurs, attempting to share the load. Immediately I spotted a problem. Each spur had a movements or radio officer whose job it was to maintain the wing's roll and record where individuals were. Clearly Blue had far less to do than Red. I detailed one radio officer to control the movement of both wings moving the spare officer onto Perrie Red. My officers from Bravo commented, "They aren't going to like it," adding, "they have an easy time sat around on Blue."
"Exactly my point. Now there will be five officers detailed Red and three Blue each day."
It soon became accepted and normal, safe practice.

I put Officer Kev to work as my cleaning officer. The wing hadn't seen paint since it had opened. That was his first task beginning with all staff areas.

Our old friend Billy Tobin turned up.
"Time for a change, Tom, it's nice up here. Quiet on that Blue Spur."
Kevin told Bill that it was only temporary, he would have to move to Red Spur in a week or two.
"No, we can't have that, Kev, Bill will be employed as our wing orderly and cleaner, that way he can stay on Blue."
Bill was delighted and readily agreed.
Kevin said, "What about the waiting list?"
"I think I'm at the top, Kev," interrupted Bill. At this point Officer Paul walked in and shook Bill's hand.
"Have you sorted him a job yet, Tom?"

An exasperated Kevin replied for me. "Yep, it's all sorted. Come on, Bill, let's get you started."

Dog Training

My eight year old daughter had become obsessed with dogs. She carried her dog encyclopaedia, which was almost as big as her, everywhere studying it at every opportunity, constantly quizzing adults in dog recognition. I had owned a German shepherd before she was born and she had his pictures on her bedroom wall. It was only natural that this became her favourite breed. I was constantly bombarded with questions about the prison dogs, particularly the attack or patrol dogs, so much in fact that I phoned the dog section enquiring if I could arrange a meeting for her with one of the dogs and his handler. SO IC the dog section said, "We can do much better than that, Tom, bring her along next Wednesday for a full training day."
"She's only eight."
"Don't worry about that, she'll have a great time and so will you."

Wednesday couldn't come soon enough for her. The excitement was on a level that rivalled Christmas Day. We all met at the Mess for breakfast, then off to the sea cadets just a few hundred yards from the prison, a fantastic venue for the training day. Casey was sat positioned in the centre of the parade square surrounded by twenty German shepherds, all facing her. One by one individual handlers would release their dog and walk away. The dog was staying prone, not moving, just staring at my daughter.
"Impressive isn't it?" said the SO confidently.
It certainly was but I was extremely nervous, particularly when the SO instructed her to remain perfectly still and not move.

Then it was my turn, much to my daughter's amusement. I was dressed in a rubber suit and told to run off like an escaping prisoner when a dog would be commanded to recapture me. This resulted in me being jumped by an eighty pounds Shepherd at speed, knocking me to the ground. This exercise was repeated by all the dogs and included me shooting them with a blank firing handgun and waving a baseball bat.

Needless to say, by coffee break I felt I had gone a couple of rounds with Muhammad Ali. Meanwhile, my daughter had memorised the names of almost all the dogs but she didn't know the name of a single handler.

Then it was the turn of the drugs dogs while the attack dogs were rested. No rest for Casey and I. We had to hide drugs, alcohol, weapons and explosives in buildings, in the open and on our person. These animals, mainly labs and spaniels, were as impressive as their larger companions. We were both amazed by their skills and enthusiasm in finding the contraband we had hidden. Breaking for lunch and a well-earned rest, we headed into Evesham town centre for a bite to eat. As I dipped into my pockets to pay, I found several wraps of cocaine from the morning training session. My daughter innocently said, "Don't worry, Dad, the dogs will find it this afternoon."

It's all I know, Guv

Back on Perrie Wing a young prisoner who was well known in the traveller community had "smashed up", a term commonly known in prison often referring to the destruction of the cell and its contents. Luke Clayfield had smashed up. Attempts to talk to him at his door had failed. He was angry about not being given a job at the Labour board the previous day. Sometimes the con's anger and frustration were exhausted after a smash up but in Luke's case it most certainly was not, threatening to assault the first screw who unlocked the door and arming himself with a table leg to help in the process.

I arranged for a C&R team to be on the wing for lunch time lock up, informing the centre PO that it may be prudent to have two teams sent up, one in reserve. They both arrived just after the wing was secured and the roll given as correct. Briefing the teams, I told them that Clayfield was both armed and dangerous. This brought about a comment from one young, cocksure inexperienced officer.

"He won't be when we finish with him, SO."

I looked him in the eye and said, "Will you be going in first with the shield then?"

"No. I'm not on the shield, sir."

"Good, cause he is going to come at the shield like a madman. I know him, he is as strong as an ox and lightning fast. Do not underestimate him."

The message finally sinking in, they moved into position outside of his cell on Red Spur. I gave Luke a final chance to give himself up by talking to him myself. Opening the inspection flap on the cell door I noticed that he had stripped down to his shorts and covered himself in washing up liquid, which makes it very difficult to grip someone and apply wristlocks in a fight. Recognising me, Luke moved towards the door.

"It's nothing against you, guv, or your wing, but this is all I know," he told me raising his fists defiantly.

I told him that one day those fists would land him a life sentence.

"I know that," was the sad reply.

"Okay, Luke, you leave me no choice," I said closing the flap.

A team moved into position behind a huge officer who carried the long shield.

"Visors down," he instructed his two colleagues who closed in tight formation right behind him. A fourth member of the team slid his key into the lock, quietly unlocking to gain that split second of surprise. Immediately the door swung open. Clayfield rushed the shield which filled the doorway, striking it with so much force that it cracked. These Perspex shields were designed to take the blast from a shotgun and resist a petrol bomb. All four officers and the prisoner were on the cell floor. That too had been covered in detergent. Luke was holding his own. One officer had control of an arm but that was it. The other three were exhausted and losing what little control they had. I instructed the fresh team to take over. Eventually, they had control of his head and both arms, finally applying handcuffs. They stood him up as he gave up.

Moving to the seg unit under restraint, calmer and totally spent he said to me, "Told you, guv, it's all I know."

Career Change?

Officer Matt entered my office with a prisoner reluctantly trailing behind him.

"Tom, he says it's nothing but look at the swelling on his face."

You couldn't miss it. One side of his face was incredibly swollen, but he was looking down at the floor saying nothing.

"Have you been assaulted, mate?" I said, knowing full well that was the only reasonable explanation.

Thinking hard before he offered a reply, he said, "Yes, but it's fine." I told him that it certainly wasn't fine, explaining that I myself had experienced a broken jaw and that was what I believed his injury to be. He went on to say that it had happened yesterday but now the pain was too much to bear.

"I have to ask you, who did it?"

Clearly struggling to talk both physically and emotionally, he said, "You know I can't tell you, boss."

I wasn't expecting anything else.

"Okay, Matt, get him up the hospital."

The centre PO phoned confirming my prognosis.

"Do you want to take him to outside hospital, Tom? I've got two officers ready to go."

I agreed.

Arriving at Worcester Hospital everything went to plan and we were told the operation would be performed within the hour. The prisoner was given a general anaesthetic. Standard practice is that one officer will be in the operating theatre for the duration, dressed accordingly. The surgeon who is performing the operation is explaining the process when I tell him that I had a similar operation a couple of years earlier.

"Oh, I may well have been the guy who operated on you," he said enthusiastically adding, "fancy watching this one?"

"Yes please," I replied with equal enthusiasm.

In no time I had scrubbed and dressed up for the op. The surgeon then motions me to position myself next to him at the head of the operating table. He shows me a range of small titanium plates in a box, one of which will be selected for the prisoner. An incision is made in the con's cheek to allow a tiny drill and screwdriver to be inserted. The lip is pulled down exposing the lower part of the jaw, all very simple, quick and easy. A plate is selected, positioned over the drilled holes and then, wait for it... The surgeon hands me the screwdriver instructing me to carefully tighten up the four screws, securing the plate to the jawbone which I perform with all the skills of a junior surgeon. Job done. The surgeon congratulates me with a shake of the hand joking that I should consider a career change.

Back home at the jail the prisoner thanks me for everything. I tell him it was nothing and that I was just happy to help. Turning to walk away I tell him that I assisted with the surgery, actually securing the plate to his jaw.

"No, guv, you're kidding me, right?"

"I'm deadly serious," I tell him, explaining what happened.

He begins to smile finally saying, "Don't make me laugh, guv, it makes my jaw hurt."

Delta Wing

With the arrival of a newly appointed principal officer to Perrie Wing who made it clear to myself and SO Dave she didn't appreciate our management style, we wasted no time in arranging our departure from the wing. Dave moved to security and I to Delta Wing. SO Emma, a friend of mine, was transferring to HMP Dorchester in Dorset. I slotted straight into her role, happy to be back on an old-style wing.

Change was once again sweeping across Long Lartin. E and F Wings had been demolished and the construction of a replacement, purpose-built wing was complete. The one hundred and eighty cell house block had now been completed. Mainstream prisoners were located here. Perrie Wing and Delta. A, B and C Wings now held VP's, many of these being sex offenders, including paedophiles.

Happy to be on Delta with mainstream cons was fine, but we all knew that it would be short lived as all four remaining, old-style wings would soon house VP's. Not a prospect many of us relished.

SO Emma assisted my smooth transition before departing. A good mix of experience and probationary staff eased the process. The wing seemed steady.
Time for a morning coffee. Pushing open the back office door I was aware of hushed voices, one male, one female. As I entered the staff kitchen a young probationary female officer and a high-risk category A prisoner of a similar age quickly slid off a chest freezer that they had seconds before been sitting on extremely close to each other. Alarm bells were ringing in my head. I asked them what the hell they thought they were doing together in the kitchen with the door closed. The officer remained silent but the cat A began to "jive talk" me. I stopped him in his tracks. "Get out!" I shouted. He left reluctantly, continuing to make excuses. Embarrassed and emotional she began to express her feelings toward the con. I told her to

remain where she was and sit down while I reported the incident to security. Within the hour the prisoner had been moved to the seg unit with a view to him leaving the establishment that day. The officer was escorted from the wing never to return.

Resident Artist

Wandering into a cell on the ground floor of Delta, it was a similar experience to entering an art gallery. There were amazing examples of art on display, particularly portraits. I had always admired the skill involved in producing such works of art. The prisoner was clearly talented and enjoyed showing off his paintings. They were representations of many musical artists such as Jimi Hendrix, Elvis Presley and Kate Bush. I asked the artist if he fancied a commission for the wing. I suggested a large mural on the twos landing. Alpha Wing had a 1930s art deco style one depicting a motor car race through the Pyrenees. Charlie had the Beatles proudly displayed on their walls.

"Okay, guv, if you supply the brushes and paints... What are you thinking?"

I didn't have to think, I knew.

"The Rolling Stones," I blurted out.

"Yep, that would look cool, an album cover or a portrait of them?" he asked.

"Leave it with me, I'll get back to you."

I spent that evening trawling through my old vinyl collection. I knew what I was looking for, the 1976 album entitled "*Black and Blue.*" The following morning I showed him the album cover.

"Brilliant, a picture of the band on the album itself."

He got to work that afternoon. Work continued on and off for six weeks, much to everyone's interest, fascination and general discussion. The finished result was excellent and became a focal point of the wing. He signed and dated it with a line to me that read "Commissioned by Senior Officer Tom Hill. Delta Wing." I felt very proud.

Judgement Day

Judgement day arrived. The last of our mainstream prisoners had finally moved off the wing to allow vulnerable prisoners to take up residence. Some of the new receptions were in debt, victims of bullying, poor copers etc. However, the majority were sex offenders and paedophiles. These were prisoners who were in denial of their offence and as such would not participate in any form of offending behaviour programmes. Many were historical offenders who were claiming their innocence and not accepting the sentences handed down to them by the courts. They were often elderly, creating problems that an ageing population brings. One officer remarked, "He just looks like my grandad."

I pulled her up instantly, reminding her why he was here.

"Go read his file. It's fucking disgusting."

For many of them the internet had been their downfall, enabling them to be caught and prosecuted. As the wing began to fill, the shocking truth of the crimes began to surface amongst us. It was extremely difficult for us all to adapt and adjust quickly to our new clientele, particularly those with years in the service who, like myself, had little dealings with these types of prisoners. Long Lartin had not been designed or built for them either.

They were not violent offenders and had no intention or means of escape. It soon became apparent that most, if not all, were enhanced status prisoners under the IEP scheme. They were generally compliant and well behaved causing us no problems, the majority having arrived from HMP Wakefield, often referred to by other cons as "Monster Mansion". Their refusal to accept guilt and non-compliance towards any offender behaviour work deemed their IEP status should be urgently reviewed and downgraded accordingly. I raised the issue with the head of res at the earliest opportunity. She appeared dismissive and reticent. I pushed my point of view.

"Just because they are not a control problem and obviously caused no issues at Wakefield doesn't make it right. They breach national IEP policy and should be downgraded."

The res gov clearly didn't appreciate me calling her out in front of other SO's and PO's present at the residential morning meeting.

"Enough. I will speak to you after this meeting, Tom," she ordered.

I couldn't wait.

Meeting concluded, I remained behind. She appeared more relaxed now, though I wasn't about to let it drop.

"It's not just Delta, we have around two hundred VP prisoners in this jail now who are enhanced status. It's wrong."

"I don't want any problems on the old wings with them. Do you understand?"

"No, I don't. They aren't capable of giving us a problem."

"Tom, this meeting is concluded."

With that she logged onto her computer. I stormed out leaving her office door wide open.

Extremely frustrated, returning to Delta to inform the troops, I struggled to comprehend her reasoning. All I could come up with was she didn't want to upset anyone by simply challenging prisoners. But that was her job after all.

With the weekend fast approaching I decided to act alone. I had the authority to downgrade after all, so why not?

On Saturday morning I briefed the staff of my intention. The cons would be called into my office one at a time, challenged and downgraded if they failed to meet the policy. I wasn't expecting any problems. Officer Kerry had volunteered to assist and she called up their files individually as we began to interview. The contents were truly shocking. After the first half dozen who were all downgraded we had to take a break. Over coffee I asked her if she was happy to continue knowing how difficult it was for both of us, particularly for her as a young mother.

"It's okay, Tom, this is the least we can do."
I knew exactly what she meant.

They all told similar stories, all denying guilt. Some stated they had lodged appeals against conviction, yet were unable to furnish details such as a current registered appeal number. Others simply said, "It's a pack of lies, all made up," or similar statements to that effect. Most shocking of all, one con, whilst claiming his innocence stated, "It's my daughter so I did as I pleased, SO, that's my right."
He paused and then smiled. I flew at him, grabbing him to physically throw him out of the office. He was still attempting to justify himself as I slammed the door in his face. Officer Kerry and I stood stunned, looking at each other in silence. Eventually she spoke.
"I think we should stop until tomorrow, don't you?"

The following morning we ploughed on. Officer Kerry told me that she could not get the previous day's events out of her head and she hadn't slept well. Again, I asked if she was willing to go on.
"I can always get another officer to take over."
"It's my job. Besides, we are almost done," she replied.
I wasn't sure if it was anyone's job.

As the weekend drew to a close, we finished. Over fifty prisoners had been dropped from enhanced to standard with only three completing an appeal form. Emotionally drained and feeling immense satisfaction with what we had achieved, I didn't feel that the residential governor would share my view.

I wasn't wrong.

At the res morning meeting and armed with my evidence, I directed my speech toward the residential managers, especially those who ran VP wings. Sensing rebellion, she cut me off mid flow.

"What if there had been trouble over the weekend on your wing with minimum staffing levels? You should have at least waited."

I informed her that the only trouble that we encountered was having to read their awful records and listen to pathetic excuses. This brought the support I was after, other wing managers now offering their approval. Finally, she caved in agreeing that all VPs should have their IP status urgently reviewed.

Hallelujah!

Hospital Visit

Word reached me that Billy Tobin had been badly assaulted on Perrie Wing by a group of Muslim prisoners who had objected to the open display of his faith. Bill was a practising Buddhist. He enjoyed the peace, calmness and sense of wellbeing it brought him. Often, he would be seen cross-legged in a trance-like state in his cell or on the exercise yard. His party piece was standing on his hands propped up by the fence in the yard, meditating. It always brought amusement and interest from others. This time the interest was not welcomed.

I went to the prison hospital to see him. He was in good spirits despite his beating, a fractured cheekbone and a bruised and swollen face. He looked a mess and looked in pain.
"Fucking hell, Bill, you have to get off that wing," feeling the anger toward his attackers build up inside me as I spoke.
"No, it will be fine," he said, attempting to move in bed as he spoke.
"Come to Delta with me, you can be the office orderly as you will be the only straight goer on there," I joked. As he laughed the pain washed over him again. "I'm serious, Bill."
It was like talking to my dad, yet Bill was only about ten years older than me.
"I can't live with them wrong 'uns, Tom. You understand, don't you?"
I did.

They Think it's all Over – It is Now!

A major drama in my personal life was unravelling which would ultimately affect my career as a prison officer.

I was having an affair with another prison officer on Delta. Katie was twenty years my junior. After six months it all blew up over a weekend off. Her husband, a police officer, had suspicions but she spelt it out to him and left. The first I knew of it is when the estranged and very angry husband is bashing in my front door at two thirty in the morning. He confronts me in my hallway as I open the front door. My then wife has no idea. The only way the ugly and sad confrontation de-escalates is when my fourteen year old daughter comes downstairs woken by the shouting. She asks what's going on and if the unwelcome stranger is drunk. I tell her, "No, he isn't, he is just angry." Her innocent presence unsettles him and he leaves. My wife hysterical, my daughter confused and in tears, I leave shortly afterwards.

On foot I make my way to a friend's house, another Delta officer, careful to avoid the angry cop who is lurking in his car around the village. Katie is there waiting, so too are the police who have been called as a result of his threatening demeanour and behaviour. They advise us both to leave the area. We agree. I apologise to them and express some sympathy towards their colleague. To my surprise they are not supportive of him. "What has happened does not justify his actions toward either of you."

We check into a hotel for the weekend happy to finally be together. However, Katie is generally scared of her husband. She is reassured by an inspector who calls on the Saturday that he has been locked up to cool down for twenty-four hours. I thank him and say that we don't want him to lose his job.
"Oh, he won't, he just needs a cooling off period."
I always thought it a strange comment, knowing full well if roles were reversed my job would be in jeopardy.

161

The prison call to warn me that he had to be escorted from the gate lodge and off the government facility by the duty governor assisted by a patrol dog and his handler. Again, I find myself apologising for his increasing erratic behaviour. The duty gov attempts to reassure me.

"See you both Tuesday, Tom, stay safe."

I find myself replying, "Don't worry, his colleagues have locked him up for everyone's, including his own, safety."

I don't think he believed me.

Two weeks on, pressures are enormous for all parties. We are living at Katie's mum and dad's just outside Kidderminster, a seventy-mile round trip to work. Katie has to seek an emergency court hearing to gain access to her daughter and my wife is on sick leave from the service with Katie about to join her. Worst of all, my daughter is refusing to speak to me.

It all comes crashing down spectacularly when I attempt to phone my daughter from the night patrol office on Delta Wing on a cold, dark December afternoon. She promptly hangs up after a very tense and brief conversation. I'm emotionally crushed. Looking back, I was on the verge of a breakdown. I should have reported sick. Whilst attempting to get my emotions under control in order to carry on my duties, the door crashes open.

The duty governor instructs me to report to the number one governor's office. Dazed and confused I simply follow behind her saying nothing. The cold air strikes me as we walk outside towards the admin block bringing me back on point.

"What's going on?" I demand.

She says nothing. I am led into the corruption and prevention unit office (CPU) which just adds to my confusion. Forms have been hastily assembled on the desk. A clearly embarrassed principal officer begins to speak. I've got it, they are going to suspend me. I stop proceedings and do it for them, unclipping my utility belt, throwing it onto the desk along with my badge

and ID. It takes out all the paperwork ending up on the floor. There is stunned silence from both the duty gov and PO.
"What the fuck are you suspending me for anyway?"
The gov composes herself.
"For being asleep on duty!" she yells.
"What are you talking about? I was phoning my daughter."
"In the dark?"
"Yes."

My suspension from duty on full pay lasts five months and no contact or support is officially offered during that time, just the massive unofficial support from mates and colleagues right across the jail.

Finally contact is made by the CPU governor. It is not the contact or news that I was expecting. He tells me over the phone after I have to call him back. "You will be charged under the Code of Discipline with gross misconduct," almost relishing his words. (Remember the ex-dog handler, over promoted to Bravo Wing governor, Officer X Part 3.)
"The date and details of your disciplinary hearing will be posted to you."
I attempt to question him but he will not engage with me. I'm stunned, standing alone in my kitchen.

Gross misconduct. My God!

I desperately seek out my copy of the *Code of Discipline*. It clearly states that such a charge should be applied for the most serious breaches of conduct. Assault, theft, trafficking etc. If found guilty under the Rule of Probability it carries heavy penalties. I make contact with my POA union rep telling him I am not guilty of anything but doing my job to the best of my ability, despite the serious stress. Sympathising, he suggests visiting a GP for mitigation. I'm not keen. It makes me feel weak and that in some way is an admission of guilt. However, I take his advice with nothing to lose.

The doctor calls me into his office and I attempt to shake his hand. He declines the offer explaining about some virus doing the rounds. I explain my situation adding that I am fine and that my union advised the visit and apologised for taking up his time. After listening to my story he is far more sympathetic towards me.

"So, you are over fifty, going through what sounds like a traumatic divorce, living in a strange town, suspended from work and have no support?" He pauses. "You are in a very high suicide bracket. Have you had any suicidal thoughts?"

"No, doctor, but thank you for asking."

As I go to leave he tells me to make an appointment at any time even though I am not registered at the practice. As I thank him he wishes me good luck and extends his hand to shake mine.

The date for my disciplinary hearing is set. It will be conducted by the new governing governor of Long Lartin who I have never met. My POA rep informs me that he has a somewhat ruthless reputation but has only been at Lartin a week.

I arrive dressed in a suit and clinging to a file of written supportive evidence, not that it makes any impression. This governor has his mind set even before we begin. He calls the duty governor who alleges me being asleep that afternoon. When I question her she cannot look me in the eye. I suggest she is mistaken; it was dark and I shouted at her when she entered, adding that if I was a prisoner in crisis I would have been offered support. Stopping short of calling her a liar, I allow her to respond.

"I think he was asleep, sir," directing her answers to the number one who in turn asks if she knows of my personal situation.

"No, sir."

My PO rep reacts immediately.

"With respect, ma'am, that is utter rubbish. The whole jail was aware of what was going on in Tom's life."

She says nothing, staring straight ahead as if waiting to be steered by the governor. It works.

He says "enough" and thanks her for her time.

She makes a hasty exit despite protests from my rep who then asks for a break in the proceedings. Even this is argued by the number one who eventually concedes.

"This isn't going well Tom. His mind is made up and he simply won't listen to reason. Prepare yourself for a written warning. We can appeal his decision and award."

Agreeing, we reconvene.

He had reached his decision.
I prepare myself.

As he begins to deliver my fate he stands and leans across his desk towards me in an intimidating and threatening manner. He says the words that nothing could ever prepare me for.

"I am going to dismiss you from the prison service."

My rep jumps up immediately and takes my arm, along with the governor's secretary who is equally shocked.
I stand directly facing my judge, jury and executioner.

"Don't worry, I've got this. I know exactly what he wants. A reaction, it's all on tape. Let's go and bring the paperwork for the appeal."

I am guided into the governor's secretary's office. The pair appear less in control than myself.

My rep finally says, "Tom, he has made an example of you. You are a popular and long serving senior officer. No one will dare cross him now."

The secretary nods in agreement adding, "I'm so sorry, Tom, you must appeal this."

Outside of the jail Officers Katie, Paul and Bob are all waiting for me. When I break the news to them there is utter and complete disbelief followed by shock. Katie is in tears. Paul drives us to a pub near his home. We make camp there well into the evening. Officers Brian, Mike, Big Nige and Matt have joined us. The drinks have numbed my shock and eventually most of my thoughts.

The following morning I wake up early in Paul's house when the reality of the previous day's events hit home hard.

Four weeks later my appeal is to be heard by the head of the high security prisons estate in London.

London Calling

Our first hurdle is getting to London. My union rep presents our rail warrants that have been issued by the prison to the ticket master at the railway station in Evesham who regrets to inform us that they are not valid for "provincial travel". We have to pay with Katie's credit card. The train dumps us at Paddington. Making our way past Big Ben and the Houses of Parliament, I realise I have come to the corridors of power for my fate to be decided.

Entering 102 Petty France Street in the City of Westminster, we are escorted to the top floor. We are made welcome and put at ease right away. They are clearly ready to begin.
"Take your time. Unpack your documents and we will proceed when you are ready."
The atmosphere is formal yet relaxed. I notice they have the new *Code of Discipline* laid out before them. I had been charged months earlier under the old outgoing manual. My union rep notices it too. We say nothing. I just wanted my job back.

Repeating my story again they appear sympathetic but more importantly are listening to the detail. I conclude that I hope that I am not judged morally as well.
"You will not be judged on moral grounds, that I can assure you."
Continuing, he says, "We the prison service have a duty of care to our staff and it is clear that in your case we have let you down badly. We will write to you within two weeks informing you of our decision."

On the journey home I am in a buoyant mood confident that the appeal had gone well.
Then reality strikes.
"You may have to move prisons as our governor may view your position at Lartin untenable," says my POA rep.

The two weeks awaiting a decision drag on. Even my postman has been briefed. He rings the doorbell and says, "I think this is what you have been waiting for," handing me an official-looking recorded delivery envelope, postmark London.

We stand outside the flat together in the sunshine saying nothing, just both staring at the envelope. I break the silence telling him I had to go inside to read it.

"Of course. Good luck."

Upstairs I turn David Bowie down to a whisper, telling myself to man up and open it. There are two full pages of text. I quickly scan over it.

YES. Appeal upheld. RESULT.

To be reinstated at HMP Long Lartin. RESULT.

At the rank of prison officer. WHAT THE FUCK?

They have busted me down. I'm fucking angry now. Reading the detail about their "duty of care" and lack of it blah blah, the phone rings. It's the prison. They have clearly been informed of the outcome before me. The duty governor (the same one who supervised my suspension) asks when I will be returning to work. I remind her that I had been sacked from the service six weeks ago and as a result I have had to sell my car. Silence.

She then says, "I didn't mean for this to happen or for it to go this far."

"Well it fucking has!"

I hang up.

Katie arrives at the flat ecstatic.

"How do you know?"

"It's all around the jail. You have been reinstated at Lartin, you've got your job back."

"Yeah, but they have busted me down."

She doesn't get it, only wanting to go out and celebrate.

One Flew Over the Cuckoo's Nest

A week drifts by before I am ready to return. Putting on my uniform was incredibly difficult. I don't even have the appropriate rank insignia. My spirits are lifted however when I walk into the jail. Handshakes, hugs and endearing comments everywhere. It's humbling. There is a notable absence of support though from senior management.

No one speaks to me until I request a meeting with the deputy governor some two weeks later. It is clear they are actively avoiding me. She, the dep, tells me that my situation "just spiralled out of control until it was too late." The phrase "duty of care" is mentioned again. I tell her the service is simply paying lip service to it.
"If this new culture of suspension continues within the service unchecked, there will be serious casualties."

The prison clearly doesn't know what to do with me or where to place me. I end up working in the prison hospital, appropriate really as this is where many prisoners who are not necessarily physically ill are located. There is simply no suitable accommodation for them elsewhere.

During my time working "upstairs" the hospital held Radislav Krstić, a Bosnian war criminal, who was serving a thirty-five year sentence, reduced from forty-six years on appeal, for his part in the killing of Bosnian Muslims in Srebrenica in 1995. The former major general, convicted of genocide involving approximately eight thousand Muslims was not going to be located anywhere but our prison hospital, along with half a dozen other misfits. The roll never made double figures.

Krstić was eventually moved to HMP Wakefield where three men, all practising Muslims serving life sentences, entered his cell and slashed him with blades. He suffered severe wounds to his face and a five-inch slash across his neck. All three were charged with attempted murder. The prosecution claimed that the motive for the attack was one of "punishment or revenge". Indrit Krasniqi, Iliyas Khalid and Quam Ogumbiyi were found guilty at Leeds Crown Court, not of attempted murder but of wounding with intent to cause grievous bodily harm. Krstić had told the court he thought he was going to die.

I was left alone to run the regime with another officer, often Big Nige, so it suited me fine. Some of the patients were mentally disturbed and dangerous. Mad and Bad. We had to be alert around them. Humour was often the best remedy and Officer Nigel was an expert at administering it to the patients, enabling us to all get along.

With time I began to settle into a routine. I had been offered a retrial by my union but even the phrase filled me with dread.

Gymnasium

An opportunity presented itself in the prison gymnasium. I had wanted to work there over twenty years earlier. One door closes and another door opens. Initially, it was a part-time position helping out in the evenings and weekends. I loved turning my hand to new sports and fitness regimes. I would actively participate, referee, organise and supervise whatever was required. My overall wellbeing and fitness levels improved dramatically. I still wasn't a fan of weight training but there was now much more focus on core exercise and activities that suited me. It didn't take long for a full-time position to become available. I applied and was interviewed. My age and fitness levels were questioned by the PO PEI. I didn't even have to answer, the PEIs replied for me in unison:
"We all want Tom, and he is fitter than most in this jail."
I was blown away by their unwavering support.
The job was mine.

I was rushed off to an intensive first aid course and then a residential PE course at Lilleshall National Sports Centre in Shropshire.

Lilleshall National Sports Centre

On my arrival, dressed in a suit and sat at the back, I was mistaken as a governor visiting the centre. It wasn't until the coffee break that the other students realised that I too was on the course. They didn't expect many fifty year-olds. When I said I played football there over twenty years earlier for the prison service, one of them said that they were not even born then.

"No offence."

"None taken."

Everything was covered from refereeing to diet and nutrition. Sports I had little interest in, such as volleyball now appealed. We were instructed to organise, participate and referee a hockey tournament one afternoon, the next badminton. It was during this badminton tournament that I was totally humiliated. The draw had been made and I was up against none other than the national champion of the service. I was thrashed 21-1 in front of a packed sports hall. The only reason I scored a single point was because I mishit the shot and it fell over the net to cheers and applause from the crowd. We shook hands and he congratulated me on being a good sport.

That evening I watched a gymnastic display by Beth Tweddle who went on to win a bronze medal at the 2012 Olympic Games in London. She had already won gold at the World and European Championships, plus the Commonwealth Games. In the bar after, surrounded by photographs of the 1966 England World Cup winning squad who had been based at the centre two weeks prior to the tournament, I felt a sense that things had finally turned around.

Life Goes On

One freezing winter evening I was in a pub with Officer Paul in Studley near Redditch. We were the only customers present except a lone individual stood at the bar. We had been watching football on the large TV screen. As it finished, Paul moaning about West Brom's performance, he casually mentioned that I may know the stranger standing with his back to us at the bar. I looked up at the stocky figure.

"No, Paul, who is it?"

He thought for a moment just as the Man United goals that sunk West Brom were being replayed adding to his misery.

"My dad was talking to him for ages the other week."

Paul's dad was a retired prison officer.

"I don't know him but you might. Hickey, that's it, Vinney Hickey."

I was on my feet heading toward the bar before Paul had finished his sentence.

"Excuse me, mate."

He turned around to face me. As he did I went to remove my woollen hat thinking he may not recognise me wrapped up against the cold. After all, it was twelve years or more since we last met "inside".

"Tom, you haven't changed a bit, you look exactly the same. What are you drinking?" he said laughing.

We chatted for a while with me calling Paul over to join us in my round. What struck me on reflection was the way Vinney talked about his eighteen years in prison with almost a fondness and without bitterness. He talked about screws and cons as if they were old friends and I guess some were. I'm sure he was well practised at blocking out the dark times, of which there were plenty. Vincent Hickey finally had his conviction overturned by the Court of Appeal in February 1997.

Gym Part 2

Finishing the gym course at Lilleshall I was required to undergo an independent fitness test at HMP Hewell, Worcestershire. Turning up at 6.30am there was a guy working out, a suit flung over an Olympic bar.

"I'm just off," he said racing to collect his suit.

I told him not to rush, I was just very early for a fitness test. He seemed to relax asking me what prison I was from.

When I told him Long Lartin he said, "How is your fucking number one governor getting on?"

I was guarded with my reply.

"He hasn't done me any favours."

As he left the multi-gym, walking towards me he whispered, "The man's a cunt, he's narcissistic." Raising his voice now, "I was on his management team at Belmarsh, he treated us all like shit."

Wow. I wasn't expecting that.

"Funny you should mention it, he is the sole reason I am here. Have you time for a coffee and a story before you go?"

He did. When I had finished my tale we shook hands and he wished me luck.

Arriving back at Lartin with a renewed focus and direction, I was looking forward to my new job. I wouldn't be disappointed.

My first weekend now employed in the prison PE department full-time was spent with PEI Kev on the Astroturf for football. I offered to referee the match but Kev wouldn't hear of it.

"You play, Tom, then you will finally have made it as a professional footballer," he joked. "Just relax now, you have done your time, you can train and participate in sport here as you please," a sentiment encouraged by the other PEIs. "You are a legend in this jail and they can't take that away from you."

"Big Nige said I was yesterday's news and today's fish and chip paper," bringing us both back down to earth laughing. I reminded Kev how I and my staff felt a sense of relief in the dark days on Bravo Wing a few years previous, when he and all the PEIs arrived on the wing to back us up. Bravo Wing at boiling point. They offered to do whatever was needed. I hadn't forgotten the support that day, it was as if the cavalry had arrived.

Kevin, who I was replacing, would be embarking on a new career with Forest Green Rovers Football Club, then of the National League. He had agreed to join as their goalkeeping and conditioning coach. Later that season I met him at Bristol Rovers. They were playing Forest Green and during the warm-up he ran over to chat for a minute, much to the amusement of the home fans. He told me how much he was enjoying the move from the prison service, travelling to stadiums like ours. I wished him luck. We lost 1-0.

PEIs are often criticised for having a closer relationship with prisoners than their colleagues in black and white. It is understandable, though most realise they are prison officers first and foremost and gym screws second. My relationships were mixed. Prisoners who didn't know me were fine, those who had known me as a senior officer would tend to keep their distance initially. As we have discussed previously, sport breaks down barriers. Some cons still addressed me as a senior officer of the PE department, even the chaplain could not break the habit.

It wasn't all fun and games. I found myself having to supervise the bowls competition among the older paedophiles. I wasn't happy, expressing my thoughts saying that I certainly wouldn't be actively joining in by playing for a team which was regarded as the norm. My fellow PEIs were quick to tell me that I was happy to play cricket with the terrorists at weekends. What was the difference? I conceded they had a point.

Festival of Eid – Muslim Extremists Radicalisation Part 2

After a month of abstaining from food and water, Muslims around the world celebrate the end of Ramadan with a feast. It is no different in a maximum security prison. This is known as the festival of Eid Al-Fitr. Eid is Arabic for feast or festival.

The numbers of Muslim extremists, Muslim converts and mainstream Muslims had swelled dramatically at Lartin. Fearing a flashpoint in the prison chapels it was decided that the most practical space to hold Eid was the gymnasium. The gym staff would be supported by discipline officers. The security department thought it better if just the gym staff were in the main sports hall during prayer to alleviate any tensions. The taking hostage of a prison officer with a view of execution was now deemed a very real threat within the service, even if government and Home Office officials were playing it down. Incidents at other top security jails of this nature had been attempted, thankfully however they had been averted by quick thinking staff and individuals. We now had a terrorist monitoring unit within our security department. Frustratingly, they appeared to be doing just that – monitoring – with little or no direct action to address the issues. There were suggestions at government level for Muslim extremists to be held separately at establishments to avoid the radicalisation of others. Yet again it failed to materialise.

The previous weekend I had witnessed two examples of such radicalisation for myself whilst taking names at the gym door. Not looking up from my list an Islamic name was muttered that I wasn't familiar with. On gazing up at the individual who I knew well, often discussing and playing football together, I recognised the Manchester City shirt but not the shaved head and long beard. He didn't speak to me or make eye contact, just pointing to his new name on the sheet.

At the terrorist cricket session, as we referred to it on Sunday afternoon, an elderly prisoner who I had known on and off for years arrived.

"John, I didn't know you played cricket," I said naively.

Sheepishly he replied, "I've got no choice, Tom. I do cooking and cleaning for them too."

He struggled to hold the cricket bat and was out first ball.

The iman and PEI Sid vacuumed the hundred or so prayer mats that had been brought from the chapel. Food had been prepared and delivered by the kitchen staff. Later that morning one hundred and forty prisoners arrived dressed in their finery to celebrate Eid. One officer remarked as they all knelt to pray,

"I wish I had a camera, no one would believe this sight in a British high security jail."

Officer X – The Finale

Supervising an evening racquetball session, a prisoner who I often played short tennis with approached me. I asked him if he wanted a game. He said he didn't. He had only come to the gym that evening to escape the noise and politics of his wing.
"Fine by me," I told him.
We then sat on a bench together watching the action on the courts. After a period of silence as if he was trying to remember his lines, he spoke.
"Mind if I ask you something?"
"Yep, go ahead," not really sure what to expect.
He had overheard other cons discussing the fact that I had once been a senior officer. Apparently, they had been on Bravo Wing at the same time as myself. It was then he realised who I was. I was intrigued and I encouraged him to continue his story.

He explained that at HMP Full Sutton in Yorkshire he had met both prisoner Y and Officer X and knew them both well. Especially prisoner Y. They had, as he put it, "been in business together" in the jail. He had met Officer X after her resignation from the service on her prison visits to prisoner Y after his move there from Long Lartin, even being best man at their wedding in the prison chapel. He said there had been a falling out between himself and prisoner Y and that was why he had been moved south to us. I wasn't sure if that part was true. I did know their marriage had been allowed by the prison authorities. We both discussed how on earth "they" had ever sanctioned it, with me adding that she should never have been allowed to visit, let alone marry in prison.
In full agreement he said, "Don't worry, she won't be visiting anymore, they have split up. She ripped him off good and proper."
This I wasn't aware of.

The tables had turned, the student had finally become the master.

Back to the Future

I had hoped to finish my career in the gymnasium. Looking forward to retirement all good things come to an end however, and the service was entering a new era of cuts and austerity. Overnight redundancy packages were offered and many experienced staff left. The official Home Office title of their latest venture was "Fair and Sustainable". We called it "Unfair and Unsustainable" which proved to be correct in the long term. Lartin had to move staff around to plug the gaps. Regimes were cut back drastically, including the gym, resulting in me having to put on black and white for one last time.

Arriving back briefly on Alpha before moving to Bravo I was, to be honest, disinterested. I was just marking time toward my own release date in 2020, my sixtieth birthday. I had managed both these wings with a clientele of mainstream prisoners back in the day, so being told what to do by vastly inexperienced managers was a very difficult pill to swallow. It took me a long while to settle into the regime, the service having changed beyond recognition from when I had joined. I struggled with a lack of decision making, direct action, bureaucracy and the PC brigade. I was viewed now by many as a dinosaur who should have taken the government payoff, yet when things got rough it was our experience and expertise they called upon.

There were the usual disturbances in the day-to-day existence of the wing. Mental illness and as a result acts of self-harm were notable by their increase, again a reflection of what was happening in the wider community.

On an evening duty playing pool with a prisoner on the twos landing, Officer Jo was sitting talking to another con when I suddenly became aware of an awful rancid smell of excreta. Looking up from the pool table Jo was now stood motionless, clearly in shock, covered from head to toe in liquid shit. The culprit was stood next to her gripping a large bucket, an individual who had mental health issues. He was staring at me laughing. Moving forward I told him that he would be going to the block. He ignored me completely. It was then I realised my mistake, I hadn't pressed the alarm bell, a basic error on my part. What had I been thinking? I clearly hadn't. He swung a punch at me but luckily I had anticipated it and he only caught me a glancing blow. It was enough to put me on the floor though. Desperate now to get to my feet and hit the alarm bell, I was in trouble when I felt his kick catch my thigh. Then, as if out of nowhere, a prisoner came to my rescue taking the perpetrator clean out across the pool table, holding him in a bear hug, allowing me to get to my feet and sound the alarm. Staff responded and dealt with the assailant pinned over the pool table while I put Officer Jo under a shower on the twos landing recess. Despite her ordeal she managed to joke with me saying, "Don't be thinking I'm going to undress in front of you." Laughing, I shoved her into the showers. She continued, "Get me a towel before the whole prison fricking sees me."

The prisoner who came to my rescue moments earlier and prevented me getting a good kicking had only recently moved from another wing after a disagreement. I knew him from volleyball sessions and thanked him for his help. He was to be rewarded days later with his transfer request being honoured.

The deranged prisoner who had attacked us both ended up in court months later, yet due to his mental state it was deemed "not in the public interest to proceed".

The wing was full of misfits and oddballs who just didn't fit into society and were in most cases extremely dangerous. Richard Baker, dubbed the "Bodmin Rapist" by the press, one of Britain's worst serial rapists who grew up in Cornwall, was given four life sentences for thirteen attacks in 1999 at the Old Bailey. Police believe he could have raped more than a hundred women. He was a good-looking, intelligent charmer who spent his summers working in Spain as a DJ. In reality he was one of the most prolific rapists police had ever known, preying on teens and young women in their twenties.

John Cooper, the Welsh serial killer who in 2011 was given a whole life tariff for what the media called the "coastal path murders", was an awkward, patronising and arrogant individual. In 1989 he had appeared on the television game show *Bullseye*. This footage later helped bring about his conviction.

Others located on Bravo had fallen foul to Muslim gangs on the mainstream wings. Two young cons from Bristol who I affectionately called the "Bristol Massive" had stood up to them with frying pans at the ready to defend themselves. They were moved for their own protection. Speaking to them it was for the protection of their attackers. Another drama averted.

Then there was Jason Marshall, a real Walter Mitty-type character. He had a bizarre history of impersonating police officers, ticket collectors, special constables, anyone in a position of authority that would allow him access to his victims.

Posing as an MI5 agent, he killed Mr Fasoli in his flat in London. To cover his tracks he set fire to the building and fled to Rome, Italy, using the victim's bank card to fund the trip. There he continued where he had left off, murdering a second man and attempting to kill another. On this occasion he was posing as a British Embassy official complete with pistol, utility belt, pepper spray and truncheon. He was quickly apprehended in Italy and imprisoned for his crimes.

For almost two years the murder in London was believed to have been an accident, Mr Fasoli having died from accidental smoke inhalation caused by the fire that had burnt down his home. It was not until his nephew discovered a hard drive in the burnt out remnants of the flat which contained webcam footage of the entire murder.

Marshall was extradited to Britain where he was sentenced to serve a minimum of thirty-nine years in 2017. Another "life in the max" at HMP Long Lartin. The only positive I can take from this shocking and appalling crime was that Marshall would often tell me that life was much tougher for him in an English jail as opposed to an Italian one. I was also able to practise my Italian language skills on him, much to the amusement of Bravo's residents and staff.

Orderlies

Matt was a prison orderly, trustee, red band, however you refer to it, on Bravo Wing. I knew him from my time in the gymnasium. He had been employed there in a similar role and it wasn't hard to see why. He was likeable, calm and trustworthy despite serving a life sentence for murder. The way he conducted himself with his peers was to his credit. He knew every prisoner's first name on the wing and would treat them all with equal dignity, respect and when required, compassion. Some officers could take a leaf out of Matt's handbook with regards to their dealings with prisoners.

Orderlies tread a fine line in their relationships with staff and cons. They cannot be seen or suspected as a potential grass. Neither can they openly support indiscipline. Matthew was excellent at balancing the two. Officer Jeff described him as a younger version of "Fletcher" (Norman Stanley from the comedy series *Porridge)*. He wasn't wrong.

Mid-morning, Matt approached me looking very serious.
"Can we take a walk, Mr Hill?"
When addressed formerly in this manner I knew something was up. He explained that some "nut job" on the wing had been paid and was prepared to stab an officer who had been throwing his authority around. There had been intel shared recently to suggest this was indeed a very real threat. Matt continued. He had spent his time since unlock "de-escalating the incident", his exact words – sounding just like a security screw. He hinted at names without naming individuals giving me just enough info to take action. He reassured me "the contract" had been lifted due to his expert negotiating skills and the inevitable settling of debts, casually adding that we may have to "skim off some canteen on Friday". I got his drift. That was his payoff.
"Oh, one last thing, Tom. We need to go outside the wing to retrieve the weapon. I have thrown it out of the would-be assassin's window."
"Nice one, Matthew."

Friday afternoon Matt and I would oversee the delivery and issue the wing's weekly canteen in our own unique style. We had it down to a fine art and prided ourselves at not being ripped off by the customers. All the banter of your local corner shop with the added spice of a potential fraud being committed at any transaction. Duvets to digestives were handed over to those who could afford it. The new prison currency had now morphed into vapes. They had replaced tobacco in line with the prison service's bid to rid itself of smoking. During my time in the service the currency had evolved from tobacco (Burn), phonecards and now vapes. All of these items were now delivered to the jail by private contractors. A prison workshop resembling a small supermarket warehouse employing forty cons would pick, package and charge the individual orders that they had received the previous week. Security was tight. The majority of items were foodstuff. No amount of "wanding" and rubdown searching was going to find items hidden down Y-fronts. There was a well-known "grass" employed in the "shop" though, Sidonio Teixeria. Tex was known to us as a highly disturbed individual who had murdered his three year old daughter and had attempted to murder his nine year old son in 2007.

Victor Castigador was infamous throughout the prison high security estate, known as a hitman and dubbed the "killer from Manila". He was serving a whole life tariff handed down to him in 1990 for two murders and two attempted murders. He had doused his victims in white spirit whilst tied up and set them alight. I knew him well from my time as senior officer on Bravo Wing. He was very pro-staff which was useful for us. I had employed him as the fish tank orderly and he took this role very seriously as we had the best kept and impressive set up in the jail. It was a huge tank full of beautiful and exotic tropical fish until disaster struck. At unlock it was discovered that all of the fish had died. Floor stripper had been poured into the tank. Victor took his revenge about a week later, taking the culprit's eye out with a pen.

184

Victor was to strike again some ten years later. In 2016 ironically, he smuggled a rock from Alpha Wing's fish tank to the canteen workshop and battered Teixeira to death. When staff responded to the alarm bell Victor immediately stopped the attack and sat quietly. At his subsequent murder trial he was quoted as saying, "I'm wrong to kill somebody but it's my job. When I was in my country (Philippines) I was a member of a liquidation squad. Sometimes you have to punish evil."
He was given another life sentence.

Victor Castigador died some six months later at HMP Woodhill of a heart attack.

Malcolm Bull, "Bully", a pleasant mild-mannered individual in his mid-fifties was the hospital prison orderly. He was always on hand to make tea and toast served with a smile and a shared joke. You would never have guessed he was doing a minimum of twenty-five years for murder. He was one of the seven members of the "Outlaws" motorcycle gang jailed for murdering a Hells Angel from London in 2007. The execution took place on the M40 as the victim was returning home after the Hells Angels "Bulldog Bash" festival in Warwickshire. It was a military-style operation with the "angel" being gunned down whilst travelling at eighty mph on his Harley Davidson.

Life in the Max

In March 2019 I am heading south with my daughter. We are on our way to watch the mighty Bristol Rovers take on crestfallen Sunderland (you're not famous anymore) in the EFL Trophy semi-final, more commonly referred to by its sponsor's name at this time the Checkatrade Trophy. We met up at Long Lartin's car park and travelled together. Expectations were high and Sky was showing the game live, an opportunity to face Portsmouth at Wembley in the final.

The rain lashed across a windswept pitch at the Memorial Ground, the floodlights illuminating standing water. There were concerns as to if the match would go ahead. It did and despite a spirited performance we lost by two goals without reply, Northern Ireland international Will Grigg being the standout player for the Black Cats and scoring their opener.

Driving back and forth on the M5 we always tuned into Radio Bristol until we could only pick up a faint signal and loads of static. The station had not only informed us of our football team's highs and lows over the years, it would also report serious news. We followed the case of Joanna Yeates, a twenty-five year old landscape architect who in early December 2010 went missing after a night out with friends in the Clifton area of Bristol. Her body was found on Christmas Day in Failand, North Somerset.

Police arrested her landlord and neighbour Christopher Jefferies. He was released without charge after three days. However, he was vilified in the media, particularly regarding his eccentric appearance. He later brought a successful libel action against eight tabloid publications over the coverage of his arrest, receiving an undisclosed sum.

The real killer, Dutch engineer Vincent Tabak, was charged on 22 January 2011 with her murder. Tabak, thirty-two, was Joanna's next door neighbour.

After a lengthy trial he was found guilty of murder in October 2011 and sentenced to life in prison, with a minimum term of twenty years. At his trial the prosecution argued that Tabak had strangled Joanna and then attempted to conceal the crime by disposing of her body. They also argued he had attempted to implicate his landlord Christopher Jefferies in the murder.

Shortly after sentencing, Tabak arrived at HMP Long Lartin to begin a life in the max.

Radio Bristol had also reported the disappearance of sixteen year old Becky Watts from the St George area of Bristol in February 2015. Travelling together that evening for our football fix I turned to my daughter and said, "I think she has been murdered." Regrettably, that turned out to be true. We listened to the details during the following months as the case unfolded. Eventually, her stepbrother Nathan Matthews was found guilty of conspiracy to kidnap and her ultimate murder, along with his girlfriend Shauna Hoare who was convicted of manslaughter. He was sentenced to life with a minimum of thirty-three years and she seventeen years. Justice Dingmans in his sentencing remarks agreed with the prosecution's belief that the planned kidnap was for a "sexual purpose".

I would have several dealings with Matthews over the following years as he was located at Long Lartin as soon as he was charged. I did my very best not to enter into social conversation with him. The way I saw it he had shamed my city.

There were no murder reports on Radio Bristol that evening thank goodness. As we reached Gloucester, heading north on our homeward journey, the signal was fading fast. We were not going to hear our manager's excuses for that evening's cup exit. My daughter turned off the radio and was looking at her phone whilst I was negotiating the fifty mph speed cameras and the heavy rain.

"Dad, there is trouble at your work. A riot! It's on the national news."

Sure enough, as we reached the jail just before midnight the scene that greeted us was one of emergency vehicles and flashing lights. There were half a dozen police cars, two ambulances and a fire engine alongside prison service Tornado Rapid Response vehicles.

It later materialised that Echo Wing had "kicked off". Staff had lost control of the situation and were withdrawn from the wing at about six o'clock that evening. The prisoners had forced them off hurling pool balls and brandishing snooker cues. Several officers had been injured and hospitalised, one with a broken jaw, and thousands of pounds worth of damage had resulted in the loss of the wing. It could have been far worse. One officer was dragged out by his colleagues who had drawn their batons to fight off a group who were attempting to take him hostage. The wing was finally retaken at one thirty the following morning by specialist Tornado Prison Service Response Teams.

The cause was levelled unofficially at one person and her rash decision making that afternoon. She, being of governor grade, had breezed onto the wing to discover an array of pots and pans lying around the prisoners' kitchen. Clearly, they were not up to the standard of her own kitchen. She ordered their removal to reception despite protests and the offer of a compromise by staff to take the offending kitchen utensils to the office and reissue them, together with a warning regarding their use and storage. They were bagged, tagged and permanently removed to reception. Staff expected a reaction when prisoners returned that evening from the workshops. They were right to do so. When informed of the governor's decision to withdraw their cooking utensils and facilities for the foreseeable future, they immediately went on the rampage. Echo Wing was out of action for three months and almost a hundred prisoners had to be relocated. The cost was astronomical.

A month later I was in reception and noticed a pile of dirty old pots and pans lying in a corner. The reception staff upon noticing my interest commented somewhat sarcastically, "Yes, that's what caused the riot."

Simon Bowman – A Sad Conclusion

Simon Bowman, fifty-four, was found dead at the flat where he was staying with his best friend Christopher Graham in High Street, Jarrow, Tyne & Wear, in May 2019. He had been brutally murdered by Graham who admitted the killing but claimed he acted in self-defence. He thought Bowman was about to rape or kill him but said he remembered nothing about the killing itself. Bowman's fingers and toes had been removed with bolt cutters and he had suffered a catalogue of injuries including thirty to his head and neck after Graham had finished with him.

He was sentenced to life with a recommended twenty-six years in January 2020. The judge said that both men had taken a "cocktail of drink and drugs" before the violence erupted.

RIP

It wasn't just prisoners who died in jail, staff did too. Officer Dave was in early on overtime for court escort when struck down by a heart attack, lucky for him dead before he hit the floor.

I carried his coffin at the funeral, one of many staff funerals that we would all attend in our number one uniforms with the Union Jack draped over the coffin. The wakes often turned lively with dozens of officers sinking pint after pint. Officer Psycho Brian asked the family at Dave's send off if it would be okay to sing "My Way" as a mark of respect to our colleague. I had already told him that I wasn't sure it was a good idea.

"I do 'My Way' better than that gangster Sinatra ever did."

He had a point. After a stellar performance the family could not thank us enough.

At Steve Selby's funeral – remember him? – Mayor of Evesham, prison taxi driver, the family couldn't thank Brian and myself enough for attending in full dress uniform at a small private affair. I told them it was an honour. There were tears all round, except Brian.

You had to watch him though.

At SO Derek's funeral we all filed past the open grave. Brian suddenly stopped in front of me throwing in a bunch of flowers one at a time. He always purchased them for these sombre occasions. He remained at attention for what seemed like ages, muttering something for Derek's ears only. At one point I thought he was going to join him. That evening we played a football match in his memory followed by an impromptu press-up competition in the middle of Wetherspoons. Derek would have loved it.

Officer Sue committed suicide. At her funeral we were late. It didn't matter as we couldn't get near the church. Staff lined the route out to the main road all saluting her coffin as it went past.

191

It was, and still is, the largest gathering at a funeral I have ever been to. So sad.

Rest in peace, all of you.

Escorting prisoners to funerals was altogether a very different experience. Security was paramount and permission to attend only being granted for immediate family and rarely for cat A's. A candle lit in the prison chapel and a prayer was the very best they could hope for.

When we did venture out security would draw up a strict itinerary covering attendance. It would not always run in tandem with the expectations of the family. They would want us to attend the wake afterwards, remove the handcuffs and distance ourselves from the service etc. The pressure was enormous. I had a standard response to their requests which was a firm "NO". The alternative was us leaving the funeral pronto.

On a trip to Liverpool, with the con giving final directions, the crowd of mourners was immense. As soon as we pulled up the car was surrounded. Steve Selby hit the central locking. The con was excellent and resolved the situation, instructing the crowd to withdraw and respect us otherwise we were off. It worked. Thanking the prisoner on the return journey for his co-operation, he replied, "Thank you, guv, most wouldn't have stopped."

Arrivederci

After more than thirty-two years in Her Majesty's Prison Service it was time to go. A retirement party was planned with Officer Brian starring as David Bowie, Freddie Mercury and Frank Sinatra (don't ask). He was also compere and quizmaster for the evening extravaganza. A three-day golf tournament with over forty officers competing had also been organised by Officer Steve. Then the world was struck with the Covid-19 virus and this country went into lockdown for the first time on 23 March 2020, the day I officially retired from the prison service.

My last weekend on duty I paid a visit to Billy Tobin. Inviting me into his cell I couldn't help but notice a family photo calendar proudly displaying a picture of his stepson John McAvoy. He made us both a cup of tea telling me he would soon be out as well (how many times had I heard those words). He scribbled down his prison number and handing it to me he said, "Thanks for all that you have done for me, Tom, now send me a postcard."
He shook my hand, pulling me in close for a hug.
"I just did my job, Bill." As I said it I knew they weren't the right words.
"Bollocks! You have been a real friend to me."
"Yeah, and you to me, Bill."
As I left the cell he shouted down the landing, "Don't forget the postcard."
"I won't," I hollered back.

Heading off Bill's wing I rounded the corner and bumped into Jetmir Bucpapa who I had got to know during my time in the gym. He was polite and smiling as always. Bucpapa, an Albanian national, had been convicted for his part in the largest cash robbery in British history, over £53 million. The raid in 2006 took place at the Securitas depot in Tonbridge, Kent. The gang left a staggering £154 million behind as they simply did not have room to take it. £32 million was never recovered.

Shaking hands, Jet told me he was being released that summer. He asked what my plans were. I told him I was off to Calabria in southern Italy, squeezed in between the Med and the mafia where I owned an apartment.

He replied excitedly, "That's where I'm heading, I have friends there."

"Not Albania?" I retorted.

"No, maybe later. Not straightaway, we can meet the mafia together," he joked.

At least I hoped he was joking.

Fast forward to summer 2020. I am sat in a beautiful piazza in the foothills of the Pollino National Park in Calabria overlooking the Tyrrhenian Sea enjoying a cappuccino having cycled up the mountain early that morning. My reason wasn't just for the views. I had a postcard to send.

The End

'One off the roll'

January 1988. My first ID Card

(SEG UNIT)

OFFICER TOM HILL
H. M. PRISON
LONG LARTIN
EVESHAM
WORCS

month. — Just 9m pleading guilty
to escaping, and an incident in
a taxi when 9 was being
arrested. — and all he, — 9, —
would like you to do, is explain
about the day out we had on
the Licence, — just to explain to
the court how 9 could of if 9
so wished escaped them, and
anything else you want to say
about that day out. — just the
truth in mitigation thats all. — its

1995. Simon Bowman's letter to me from HMP Whitemoor
after his escape and recapture. He is requesting me to be a
character witness at the Old Bailey.

I'm Duble A'd up (High Risk) and an 'E' man at the minute — unbelievable — and I don't know nothing abaut that shit up Durham Tom. — I wasn't caught or charged with anything, irrelevant of what the papers might say!! — its rubbish. Anyway Tom, have a good think abaut what I said, its all above board tənaal'opaa T!! The Bizzys must be sick as they are trying to stitch me up with a hundred and thirty thousand pounds worth of armed robberys (2) and an attempted Murder on a copper. I don't know nothing Guv! — honest!) They are barking up the wrong tree. God bless em!! :

We were ordered to remove these tie pins so as not to offend
some of the clientele.

My Service medals.

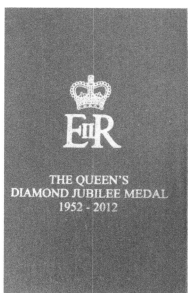 

My long service and good conduct medal awarded after twenty years of operational service.

First Words
By
Officer Paul

I'd heard of Tom Hill. I'd heard stories about Tom Hill. I'd seen Tom Hill but I had never spoken to Tom Hill. Back in 2002 I had been an officer for just over two years. One of my first senior officers was Tom's then father in law. Tom's name cropped up quite often. Some of the older officers who had worked with Tom knew him well, and most of the staff had a story to tell about him. Before I had even spoken to him I had an idea of the type of character he was.

Back then I was single, spending five or six nights a week in my local and loving every minute, well able to leave the pub at 2am and have no problem getting up for work at 6.30am. Except for one morning. I must have had a bad pint the previous evening.

I overslept. Fuck! Fuck! Fuck! I knew I was detailed a workshop that morning. With
prisoners not moving to workshops until 9am it meant I could possibly get to the jail in time. I would have to go straight to the workshop instead of reporting to Oscar 2 in the main jail. Oscar 2, the senior officer, managed the workshop move and made sure he had sufficient staff to run the shops. I would phone from the workshop to confirm my attendance. The thing was I would have to be in the workshop before Oscar 2 began the move.

Arriving at the jail, I fly through the search procedures as no one else is there as they had all arrived on time. Once through the gatehouse it's 9.05am and I'm cutting it fine. It's a straight run to the shop and only one pedestrian gate to go through. Now through the gate, running toward the workshops with my rucksack swinging over my shoulder, I'm desperately hoping Oscar 2 and his staff haven't started to make their way out to the large exercise yard that then feeds the various workshops. As the yard is coming into view, I can see one person in the middle of the yard and an officer manning each pedestrian gate.

Bad news. That is Oscar 2. This means all the workshop staff are in place except for me. They have clearly been waiting for me. The minute Oscar 2 spots me he strides towards me and looks fucked off, with his arm outstretched pointing at me holding the list of names. Before I can offer an apology, Senior Officer Tom Hill is shouting his first words to me.
"Any chance you can fucking get here on time in fucking future?" That was the day I found out Tom Hill was from Bristol.

My Twenty-Eight Years Behind Bars
By
PEI Phil

I was recently asked by my good friend and colleague to add a few words for a book he was writing. The biggest difficulty was trying to condense those words as I had so many great experiences over the years. This might come as a surprise to many who don't have prison experience.

I joined the job in 1991. My first posting was at HMP Parkhurst on the Isle of Wight. At the time this was one of the high security prisons, referred to as a dispersal prison. I completed two years as a discipline officer working on B Wing predominantly, completing my probationary period.

I had joined the job with the intention of specialising as a PEI. I had made this known in training school. On my arrival at Parkhurst, I volunteered my services to the gym. I would go in early to practise Olympic lifting, gymnastics and ball skills for all sports. On weekends off I would referee the football. This was the real test. If you could referee football in Parkhurst in the early nineties you could handle anything. I remember putting the nets up for a game one day and the buzz had gone around that it was a big game with lots of money riding on it. Prisoners would look forward to the weekend games and place bets between themselves on the outcome. Players started to arrive as the staff were doing the head count onto the yard. One side began to question where "Scouse" was. Scouse was one of the better players in the prison and a real asset to any team. It later transpired that on the way to the game he had been stabbed. All part of the plan to even up the odds. Needless to say, the game had a real edge to it.

During my six years at Parkhurst we had some very interesting staff v prisoner games.

I secured a move to HMP Long Lartin and the rest of my career was spent there.

In 2012 my world was rocked when I was diagnosed with throat cancer. I had never felt fitter or stronger in all my life. I was sat with my wife at the Queen Elizabeth Hospital in Birmingham waiting to see my consultant. He delivered the news and informed us of the treatment plan going forward. I noticed a leaflet that was appealing for people to raise money for a charity called "Cyberknife", a state of the art radiotherapy treatment. That night I contacted close friend PEI Munch and asked him to organise some charity events within the prison. It may come as a surprise to many that prisoners when pulling together for a common goal can achieve so much for various charities.

I returned to work for a few weeks before my treatment started in October 2012 and informed the gym orderlies that I would be off work for a considerable length of time. Both staff and prisoners came up with numerous ideas to raise money for the chosen charity. Prisoners did a brutal circuit lasting most of the day and I was well enough to go in and witness the event. I had lost four stone at the time and I'm not sure that everyone recognised me. I was greeted like a long-lost friend by prisoners. During my time off stacks of get-well cards from prisoners, even from cons who had moved on from the jail, arrived for me at Long Lartin. Very humbling. My family were amazed. Strangely, whilst I found it very moving, it never surprised me.

I did twenty-eight years in the service and I can't remember a single day I didn't want to go to work. I was very fortunate to work in an environment where prisoners wanted to be and enjoyed coming to. Being in a tracksuit many cons didn't even view you as being a screw. I remember doing an escort and was amazed when a prisoner I knew from the gym said in all seriousness, "I never knew you were a screw, Phil."

The staff had arranged a gruelling cycle event over two days from my beloved Leeds United Football Club ground to the prison. This was one extremely challenging ride and I had asked for it to be tough to mirror the fight that those facing cancer and the treatment they had to go through. I was quite poorly at the time so I followed the riders in my car with my wife driving. The route had some very tough climbs with many riders not completing the event until after dark.

As a result of these events, including a charity evening, almost £20,000 was raised. The Cyberknife is now in full use at the hospital.

In April 2013 I was clear of cancer and slowly recovering. I returned to work in June 2013. Then another blow. The radiotherapy had weakened my jaw and ruined my teeth. I was told that all of my teeth had to be extracted and I would have to go to Plymouth for six weeks hyperbaric oxygen therapy to strengthen my jaw. Work colleagues said I couldn't turn up to work with no teeth. I hadn't even thought of that. The long-term plan was to give me implants but I would have to wait six months with no teeth whilst it all settled down. I went through this process and did indeed return to work with no teeth. Not one single prisoner ever made a derogatory remark to me. One prisoner in the gym who I had known for years chatted to me for some time before the penny dropped realising it was me. The con was very apologetic and said he'd just not recognised me. The press loves a nasty story of prison and very rarely write good news stories about them.

I have had high-profile prisoners raise numerous amounts of money over the years for charity, one for a young local lad. His mum came into the prison to be presented with the cheque and personally thank the prisoner for his efforts. The prisoner fought back the tears as she told him what a difference her boy getting a new wheelchair had made.

I realise that a lot of what I have written is quite sombre but I can honestly say I have had some amazing laughs in the gymnasium. One short story is the time I was carrying out gym inductions, a great opportunity for a wind-up. A prisoner called Beefy, an absolute man mountain chiselled out of granite turned up. After showing him around I said, "Okay, I need to do your dental check."

He looked at me curiously.

"Due to cutbacks I have gone on a dental course to carry out these checks as part of the induction programme."

I called in one of my colleagues to take notes of my findings while I proceeded to carry out the dental check. On completion Beefy asked me if I would be able to sort out a gold cap for him. I said I could do better than that and could do the front two if he wanted. We had some spare cash in the budget. The note taker could barely contain himself.

On returning to the wing, Beefy was quick to inform his friends about how he was getting two gold caps courtesy of the prison service. One of the gym orderlies questioned him and asked who had done the induction. On discovering it was me he gave him the news that he had been had over. For the rest of his time at Long Lartin Beefy always fondly referred to me as "The Dentist".

Rachel's Story
by
Officer Rachel

My dad was a prison officer and I don't remember a point where the prison service was not a massive part of my life. I grew up on the Long Lartin prison estate, literally a stone's throw away from the maximum security jail. It would fascinate me as a child and I would constantly ask my dad a stream of annoying questions about what went on within the walls. He obviously fibbed to me about many aspects but I always found it intriguing.

There was a water tower just outside of the prison's perimeter wall. As teenagers we would climb the tower to try and see what existed within. Health & Safety wouldn't allow it these days.

Growing up on a prison housing estate was definitely an interesting experience. Prison officers of all ranks and their families lived here. This was normal for me, but in hindsight I can see it was probably unusual.

In 2009 the inevitable occurred and I joined HMP Long Lartin as a prison officer. I was only twenty-three and although prepared as best as possible for the role by my dad, I didn't really appreciate quite how unique and at times traumatic the job would be.

One example of how unique a job it was and how integral the prison service to me growing up had been, was highlighted when I met a life sentenced prisoner who would make wooden furniture in the workshops. Over the years Dad had brought home bird tables, garden benches etc. It was quite surreal at twenty-four to then be face to face with this prisoner who had known about my existence for many years whilst he was serving his sentence. I was quietly growing up having no idea I'd later be meeting him in a professional capacity. From talking to him many times I know he found the situation quite strange too.

I found myself in a number of unique situations over the years. I remember one day being on a corridor patrol, a particularly boring job and being called to security. Apprehensively, I reported to the security senior officer and was ordered to go to the segregation unit immediately as I was taking a prisoner out on escort. I was instructed to hand over my duties in the corridors to a male officer. At the seg unit I was greeted by their regular staff and told the prisoner, who was scheduled to be transferred out, was the notorious Charlie Bronson. I was relatively new in the service and had never met the infamous prisoner before. Nor could I understand why I was specifically rostered to this escort. Charlie did not want to be transferred out and was causing some issues as a result. The escort consisted of three rather large and experienced male seg officers and me. Turns out Charlie doesn't like to kick off around women, so to detail a female officer on his escort was a preventative measure more than anything else. I can say despite smothering himself in butter and needing to be restrained onto the cat A van, the rest of the escort went without issue and he was a thoroughly pleasant man, not always the man the media perceived him to be.

After specialised training I joined the prison service's national riot team aka Tornado Squad in 2011 and was fortunate to attend some pretty spectacular incidents. I remember spending seventeen hours in riots at the then privately run Birmingham Prison in 2016. The prison was operated at the time by G4S before it was returned to HMP status in 2018.

I spent four years working in Europe's largest segregation unit at Long Lartin and this exposed me to some disturbed and extremely dangerous prisoners, some who were clearly mentally unwell. I remember an incident, my dad was there too, supervising a constant watch (a prisoner at risk of self-harm or suicide). We gave the prisoner his lunch time meal at his door and he proceeded to throw the contents of it into his cell toilet and then eat it from there, instead of the perfectly clean polystyrene tray we had provided him with. Later on my dad recalled several incidents of very disturbing and degrading behaviour by this same prisoner. This prisoner was not deemed to be mentally unwell by medical professionals.

Another prisoner who we believed was also clearly unwell would not communicate the way you and I would. He would spend most of his day vigorously masturbating.

As a female seg officer within a male dominated environment you develop a quite bizarre sense of humour. We had a prisoner resident at the time who was a prolific paedophile and very outspoken about it, which aggrieved a lot of the staff. This paedophile was also trying to convince authorities that he now wanted to live as a female and had been granted permission to purchase a thong from the mail order system. The first time the male seg staff strip search him wearing this pink, lace thong was hilariously funny. This prisoner would ask me for make-up advice and I would find it quite amusing to compliment him on his eye make-up which he'd drawn on himself, very poorly, with a biro pen.

I can't explain why we had quite as much nudity within the prison environment but we did, especially in segregation. Sometimes prisoners would like to go on a "naked protest" and we had one who very much enjoyed doing that. One day he had randomly got dressed and a female governor decided to congratulate him. We opened his cell door and the prisoner was laid on his bed reading a newspaper. After the governor had congratulated him he stood up and spread his legs exposing his genitals to her. He had spent some considerable time cutting a hole around the crotch area of his trousers, only visible once he was standing. The ingenuity in itself rendered the staff in tears, maybe not the female governor though.

Segregated prisoners would often play their own tricks on me too. I remember one prisoner that I had to check on hourly. He was often completely naked, strewn across his bed, erect penis in hand, slowly masturbating. After throwing some derogatory insults his way I would continue with my work, as ultimately this happened frequently to female officers, especially in segregation. It was becoming a regular occurrence. I sent a male colleague to check on him and what a surprise this time;

fully dressed and nothing odd occurring at all. I went back to continuing my checks and then yes, back to exposing himself. My colleagues were an eclectic bunch and some of the best people I ever met in my life.

Officer Matt's Story

I was feeling pretty nervous about moving wings. I had only just finished my probation as a new officer, having spent twelve months on a very steady wing where the prisoners behaved. Bravo was anything but that from what I had heard.

It takes lots of different characters to run a prison like Long Lartin. Every officer has a different approach, different characteristics, so you just have to see how you fit in, and that takes time. Time is what everyone has in that place. As a high security prison, the minimum sentence a prisoner is serving is five years, the longest is a whole life sentence. Most of the staff are doing life too. Their working life that is, and the life expectancy for an officer after retirement is not great.

I was just about finding my way at Long Lartin, keeping my head down as I had been told to do as a new officer. I had had a very uneventful first year and now I was being moved to Bravo Wing (the Bronx) where some of the main "players" were being held. I wondered what was in store for me.

It was different to what I was expecting though. I had built it up in my head to be this madhouse. However, when I arrived on Bravo I was amazed at how relaxed the staff were and there was great banter (basically everyone being sarcastic). I loved it.

The wing was being run properly by great management and it showed in the staff. One of the senior officers, Tom, did the shift briefing on my first day. He was very likeable, had a really calming way about him and everyone listened and seemed to respect him. I would eventually find out for myself that he was the real deal, a proper old school SO who could deal with any situation, but the briefing seemed to be about who was cooking breakfast at the weekend and the football.

Everyone knew what they had to do and so everyone went and manned their stations ready for unlock. I was on the twos landing with Officer Paul. All the category A prisoners were kept on the twos as they were checked hourly at night and had to be on the same landing. We got up to the landing and sat down in the middle where we had a good view of everything. I liked Paul right away, he said "fucker" a lot. "Alright, new fucker," he said. Every other word was "fuck" or "fucker".

At exactly 8am all the prisoners' doors electronically unlocked at the same time and they started to come out of their cells to go to the recess, go and see their buddies, go to the freezers. It was a hub of activity all of a sudden. There were seventy-three prisoners on the wing and I had to start learning every name. I had heard of a few already of course, you always hear stories about the renowned prisoners. There were a few that were running this wing and Paul started to fill me in. He said it was good because they kept a lid on it. All the prisoners seemed to respect Paul and he had banter with quite a few, even the big boys. I felt like I could learn a lot from Paul and I stopped shitting myself about being on a proper wing.

That lasted a few days till the weekend and then the shit got real. That Saturday was like any other weekend, all the prisoners on the wing and out of their cells. In the week prisoners who either worked or went to education were sent off the wing and the rest were locked in their cells apart from wing cleaners, so it was pretty quiet. But on the weekend there were seventy-three prisoners milling around.

There were seven officers and the SO on the wing, one officer on the main desk, one doing movements, a cleaning officer, two officers on the twos landing and two on the threes landing. The only officer that really stayed put was on the desk. Everyone else had various other jobs to do.
Paul and I were together again on the threes landing that afternoon/evening and one of our jobs was to supervise the serving of food before bang up. We collected the trolley from

the main kitchen and wheeled it back to the wing servery. Of course, this meant that there were no staff on the threes landing and the prisoners were left to their own devices.

Unbeknown to us it was the birthday of one of the main London gangsters on the wing and a few of them had got together with some hooch and were having a party. Hooch is alcohol made in prison and can be manufactured in twenty-four hours. It's pretty horrible but does the job apparently. We constantly searched for it but it was a cat and mouse game. Wings have been known to have been destroyed by the prisoners in riots after a hooch party gone bad.

We had got wind of this before we were due to go back up to the threes. SO
Tom said, "Better not go up mob handed as it might get out of hand. Best you and Officer Paul just go and defuse the situation."
I thought he was joking. He was not. I am absolutely shitting myself going up the stairs with Paul, knowing that if this goes badly wrong we could be in some serious trouble. These are killers and gangsters fuelled up with alcohol. Paul seems cool but this is my first taste of real danger.
I'm scared.

We get up there and sure enough they are sitting down one side of the landing with the tables all pulled together, loads of nice food, and having a really good time. They see us and it goes quiet.
Paul says, "Right, fuckers, you've had your fun, hand over the rest of the hooch and that will be the end of it. Oh, and happy birthday, Dixie."

What Paul really meant was we won't nick you if you hand it over now. He was calmly offering an amnesty on the rest of the hooch to defuse the situation.

Dixie, the ringleader, reached under his table. I wondered what he was going for. I was ready to press the bell. If any alarm bell went off it was always taken seriously at Long Lartin and staff from all over the prison would race as fast as they could to the location, broadcast over the radio by the control room. I knew backup would be there within thirty seconds but a lot can happen in thirty seconds when you are outnumbered ten to one.

I'm glad I didn't as he pulled out a plastic bottle half full of hooch. Phew. He handed it over and said, "Fair play, guv." A few other bottles got handed over which we tipped away. It smelled awful. They started to get up and dispersed quietly.

Paul had handled it brilliantly. He read the situation and knew what approach to take, but more than that he had built up a respect and rapport over the last months and years with these guys, and that goes a hell of a long way.

We locked the wing up for the night with no dramas that evening but it could have been so different. I learnt a lot from Tom and Paul that night.

The Exercise
by
Officer Paul

November 1999. It's cold, wet and winter is kicking in. I am in the ECR at HMP Long Lartin, one of a team of six on duty for a day shift with Principal Officer Stuart in charge. We monitor cameras, motion detection devices, electronic gates and doors. We control the radio traffic on the net as well as other duties that include tea brewing on the hour every hour.

PO Stuart had been the training officer when I first joined a couple of years previously. At lunch time I was asked if I would go home and return for a night shift as they were short staffed. I returned at 8pm. To my surprise PO Stuart announced that he too had split his shift and would be IC of the night shift. His reasoning soon became apparent as he revealed we would be running an exercise at some point during the night. This wasn't unusual as contingency plans have to be tested. This particular exercise was a Bravo Sierra (breach of security).

Stuart asked if I was prepared to go into the grounds with a radio and keys as part of the exercise posing as an escaping prisoner. He obviously knew I was stupid enough to say yes as he had prisoner issue clothing ready for me in my size. The plan was to contact Foxtrot Wing and tell the night patrol about the exercise. When instructed to carry out a roll check they were to return an incorrect roll giving the name of Smith as the missing prisoner. The Foxtrot patrol would be the only person outside of the control room to know about the exercise prior to its commencement.

The main people involved in the exercise other than the control room staff would be night patrol officers carrying out their roll checks as quickly as they could and dog patrols. Three handlers and their German shepherds patrol inside the prison perimeter while a fourth dog team patrols outside using the prison response vehicle (PRV).

I was instructed to make my way to the green area of the prison grounds which is where the football pitch is. After about ten minutes of me leaving the control room they would transmit "BRAVO SIERRA" over the net. I was right up for this; it was going to be a good craic. Nights could be long and a bit boring so anything that made the night pass quicker was alright by me. The control room would be able to follow everything that was going on via the CCTV that covers the grounds and buildings within the prison.

It is now around midnight and I'm dressed in prison issue clothing, grey joggers and a blue/grey sweater. I have a belt on with a set of keys attached and a radio. I'm going to enjoy this.

As I set off from the control room I notice immediately that the temperature has dropped significantly since the beginning of my shift. Moving towards the pedestrian gate that will take me out of the vehicle compound and away from the administration block into the prison grounds proper, I hear it electronically unlock. The control room are watching my progress. I move through and shut the gate hearing it lock automatically. I follow the internal perimeter fencing towards the green area. This fencing is approximately twenty feet high with double rolls of razor wire running the entire length of every inch of it. There is an outer perimeter wall which is taller than the fence. I unlock another gate manually with my keys and continue to walk along the Fire Road. This is tarmacked and gives access to the whole jail for emergency vehicles. The road will take me to the green area where the football pitch is. As I move onwards unlocking gates, I'm acutely aware of how loud my key chain and keys sound in the quiet of night. It is eerily quiet. Finally, I arrive at the green area, all grassed and split into two sections. The section I am in has the observation tower that is used to monitor prisoners when they are on the association field. This section is fenced off from the football pitch. The ground is sodden and very soft underfoot following all the rain that continues to fall.

The call screeches out over the radio. "ALL STATIONS. WE HAVE A BRAVO SIERRA. CARRY OUT A FULL ROLL CHECK IMMEDIATELY AND REPORT YOUR NUMBERS TO THE CONTROL ROOM!" I realise halfway through the transmission that the volume on my radio is way too loud so I quickly turn it down so it's barely audible. Staff will be frantically entering landings on their various wings to carry out roll checks and hoping to fuck that they are not the wing to have lost one. If we have lost one we are all in massive shit. This is after all a high security jail with the best security systems in the country.

There is something not right with the transmission though. It should have begun with the warning "THIS IS AN EXERCISE". Regardless, I continue on towards the football pitch, the high mast lighting illuminating my way.

Approaching the pitch I take my keys out as quietly as I can. Unlocking the pedestrian gate I move onto the playing surface. I am now behind the newly built Perrie Wing and segregation unit. I have been in the grounds for about fifteen minutes now and I am feeling very nervous. Suddenly, I hear a gate being unlocked at the other end of the pitch. I stop immediately and can see a dog handler coming through. I turn and retrace my steps as my radio bursts into life. "JZ (control room call sign) FROM ZULU EIGHT (dog handler call sign), I HAVE SUSPECT IN SIGHT IN THE GREEN AREA HEADING TOWARDS THE OBSERVATION TOWER. I AM IN PURSUIT AND I THINK SUSPECT MIGHT HAVE KEYS." I recognise him as dog handler Tony. He clearly does not recognise me in my prison garb. He starts running towards me with his dog on the lead. I can hear the dog barking wildly with excitement and straining to be let loose so he can lock his teeth on my arm. I don't run but walk as fast as I can in the sodden ground. I know the handlers have a protocol to adhere to in these situations. They give a warning before letting the dog loose. If the dog is let off the lead I'm fucked. It would take me down in an instant and probably have half my arm to munch on as a treat for being a good boy. I don't want that so hopefully me walking means Tony won't let "Killer" off the lead. Nobody would blame him if he did release his dog. He must assume that a prisoner in the grounds in the early hours must have outside assistance for an escape. In his mind, if I get out of the jail I'm gone. Tony will know that the dog handler in the PRV will be tracking the radio traffic and be aware of my position, driving to the wall section closest to that area. Right now Tony is weighing up his options. Does he give the warning or let the dog go and guarantee I don't get out? I'm hoping it's the former and it's at this point I have become more anxious over the omission of "THIS IS AN EXERCISE" from the control room transmission. Had it been included Tony wouldn't have a decision to make and I wouldn't be shitting myself.

I get about fifty yards from the gate when Tony and Killer come through and Tony shouts, "Stop or I will let the dog go." I'm taking no fucking chances here. I don't want him to have any excuse to let Killer off that lead. I stop immediately and stand perfectly still knowing as soon as Tony gets up close and sees it's me I can stop worrying. Tony is still running and Killer still sounds as keen as mustard to get my arm. No worries, he will be close enough to see my face any second and he will twig it's an exercise. But Tony doesn't get close enough. He stops short, about twenty yards away from me, and orders me not to move.

Radio transmission. "JZ FROM ZULU ONE ZERO. I AM APPROXIMATELY ONE MINUTE FROM THE GREEN AREA." This is one of the other dog teams on his way to assist.

The radio net is busy with completed roll check numbers being confirmed to the control room. Foxtrot Wing as prearranged give an incorrect roll with no "THIS IS AN EXERCISE". The Foxtrot incorrect roll reinforces the dog handler's belief that this is the real deal.

Radio Transmission. "JZ FROM ZULU EIGHT. SUSPECT HAS STOPPED AND IS COMPLIANT. I BELIEVE HE MAY HAVE A RADIO AS WELL AS KEYS."

Zulu One Zero is now in sight and clearly knackered. He has run quite a distance to reach us. His dog seems to be dragging him along and just like Killer he is barking like fuck and straining at the leash as they head directly towards me. As they get closer I can see who Zulu One Zero is. I recognise him as an older handler but do not know him. He shows no signs whatsoever of recognising me. Within ten yards of me now he and "Wellard" pass and I am ordered to turn to my left and not move. He continues past me and is now out of sight. Having turned to my left as instructed I am now side on to Tony and Killer. I look over towards them in the faint hope that recognition will finally happen, but Tony doesn't in the shadows of semi-darkness. That's just fucking great. I start to imagine Killer and Wellard fighting over which arm they are going to have.

Zulu One Zero shouts from behind and orders me to kneel and put both hands on my head. As I do this I feel the sodden ground soak into my shaking bones. Zulu One Zero orders Wellard to stay. I'm hoping to fuck that Wellard does as he is told. He is leaving the dog there so he can handcuff me and thankfully Wellard obeys. All his training has paid off. Thank fuck. As Zulu One Zero approaches he informs me he is going to apply handcuffs and that I am to follow his instructions to the letter. He tells me to move my right hand from my head to my back and applies the handcuff, then does the same with the left. As he puts my left wrist in the cuff he whispers in my ear, "You fucking cunt." This isn't turning out to be the craic I thought it would be. Come on, Tony, get over here, look at me then tell Angry and Wellard who the fuck I am. These thoughts are rushing through my head but I daren't open my mouth. Angry is clearly pissed off as he has had to run halfway across the jail and he is not exactly svelte-like in appearance. Angry orders me to remain kneeling while he returns to fetch Wellard from where he left him. I'm then ordered to stand and start walking towards the concrete path that runs next to the inner perimeter fence of the jail. Tony and Killer approach but remain behind me with Angry and Wellard walking parallel. Tony transmits to the control room that I am handcuffed, in custody and they are escorting me into the jail. I'm really cold now, shivering, wet through and muddy. Wellard is still barking like mad and clearly wants to eat me. Angry doesn't seem to have cheered up since he got his breath back, and this becomes obvious as I try to step onto the concrete path to get out of the mud. He immediately growls, "Get back in the fucking mud."

Why did I ever think this was going to be a laugh?

Eventually, we reach the Fire Road making it easier for me to walk. I am relieved to see bright lights as I approach the jail flooding out of the open steel doors and illuminating staff that I recognise straightaway. Senior Officer Paul instantly recognises me and I see him explaining to others that this is just a fucking exercise. Angry switches onto this pretty quickly, but Tony who is further back still thinks this is all very real.

Walking into the jail Angry and Wellard follow and Tony and Killer remain at the entrance. The tension has finally eased and even Angry manages a smile. I am taken to the centre office. Had this been a real scenario I would have been escorted to segregation and strip searched. While on the centre I hear Tony and Killer arrive outside the office. Tony is clearly still none the wiser asking staff, "How the fuck did he get a radio and keys?" I walk out of the office and into the corridor and a stunned Tony looks at me in disbelief, starts laughing then calls me everything under the sun. At that very instance PO Stuart transmits, "EXERCISE ENDS."

There are howls of laughter from all the staff gathered on the centre including myself and Tony. In truth though we are both still shaken and in shock.

PO Stuart had a massive bollocking as he hadn't declared the exercise to all staff at the start. The implications could have been enormous if Tony had let Killer off in what was supposed to be a controlled exercise.

Looking back now it was great.

Officer Jeff's Story

Having worked in category B prisons at Winson Green, Birmingham, for three years and then Gloucester for seven years until its closure in 2013 due to the government's austerity cuts, I was to be transferred to HMP Long Lartin, a Cat A prison.

As soon as I arrived I found it totally different to cat B prisons. Allocated Perrie Wing, the principal officer Mike said, "You will have fun up there!" As I took the long walk those words would not be forgotten.

The wing was full of high-profile lifers in for serious crimes including terrorism. The first thing I noticed when the prisoners were unlocked was that they didn't speak to me. Previously, when I went to reception to collect a newly sentenced prisoner he would have a typical sentence of around twelve months, now when I went to reception young lads would come in with sentences of thirty years and on the long walk to the wing I did not know what to say to them.

The first week I was allocated workshops and a prisoner climbed up to the roof space, smashing his way outside onto the workshop roof itself. He wasn't brought down until later that evening and escorted to the segregation unit.

A prisoner located on the wing was autistic, and even though there was torrential rain he insisted on having exercise outside on the yard. He sat on the bench trying to light a cigarette. Some of the prisoners looked after him as he couldn't communicate very well. One evening a nurse told me that he hadn't collected his medication so I went to his cell to tell him. When I opened the cell door I realised he was dead. Two other prisoners had murdered him. Not very nice to go home late after being interviewed at length by the police. This had a big impact on me.

A fortnight later a female prison officer was escorting a prisoner off my wing to the library. All appeared well until on the way back he suddenly produced a weapon that he had concealed and began stabbing her. If it hadn't been for her screams and the brave action of two other officers she most certainly would have been murdered. This also had a huge impact on me. The prisoner was a psychopath.

In my last two years before retirement that couldn't come quick enough I was moved to Bravo, now a VP wing holding a lot of sex offenders and serial killers. Self-harming is common on these types of wings and some prisoners killed themselves whilst I was there. Moving to the wing I met Tom. I was always amazed how cheerful he was and nothing seemed to bring him down or bother him. He always seemed to fall on his feet.

Working in the jail was like being in another world, a very depressing atmosphere, like going into a house where the couple were divorcing. Having said all that I had some great laughs there. It's the humour that gets you through.

And the Final Word
by
Officer Psycho Davies, AKA Mad Brian/The General

Upon requesting Officer Psycho Davies' contribution at the completion of this book, in typical "Mad Brian" fashion this is what I received:

Three of the Ten Commandments, on reflection an appropriate conclusion to the story.

VI. Thou shalt not murder.
VIII. Thou shalt not steal.
IX. Thou shalt not bear false witness against thy neighbour (no grassing).
Taken from Exodus 20 and Deuteronomy 5.

The End

"Yes, end of, behind your doors - bang up."

"Night Boss."

Wing secure.
Prison secure.
Roll correct.

Acknowledgements

Coral.
Casey.
Lydia.
Officer contributions.
Rachel, Matt, Paul, Phil, Jeff and the General.
And anyone else who knows me.

Printed in Great Britain
by Amazon

25014277R00129